COLLAPSED

A Young Widower's Story of Hope

JOE BALDASSARRE

ISBN: 9781090936325

Table of Contents

Dedication

This book is dedicated to everyone who has supported me, guided me, and made me the man I am today, including Dennis, Nicole, Josh, Barbara, Suzanne, Darlene, Jerry, Kate, and Beth.

> "If a man knows his enemies, he will win most of the time. If a man knows himself, there are no enemies."
>
> —Lao Tzu shared by Dennis

> "Thanks to women there is humanity!"
>
> —Gerard St.-Cyr shared by Jerry

Additionally, this book is dedicated to all the spouses and partners of my friends in my support group whom I never had the honor of meeting (Jimmy, Dino, Sean, James, Doug, Gary, Eric, Eric, Alison, Chris, Chris, Joey, Rob, Alex) and those souls who left too soon, including Adam.

> "Learn from yesterday, live for today, hope for tomorrow. The most important thing is not to stop questioning."
>
> —Albert Einstein
> shared on behalf of Sean

Most important, this book is dedicated to Jen—You will always be in my heart and in the hearts of the girls, every day, especially when we are at Lifeguard Chair #6.

"We all make mistakes, so just put it behind you. We should regret our mistakes and learn from them, but never carry them forward into the future with us."

–Lucy Maud Montgomery,
Anne of Avonlea
shared on behalf of Jen
(Jen's favorite literary character)

Introduction

"Life has dark moments and it is out of our darkness that we often find our greatest beauties and strengths."

–American author Bryant McGill

Collapsed: A Young Widowers Story of Hope is about as personal a story as anyone could write. It is the story of my gradual rise from grief following the sudden death of my 35-year-old wife, a woman whom I adored and with whom I had shared a life of optimism and hope.

The book describes my evolution as I learned to rejoin the world and start living again, but now as a widower with five-year old twin daughters. I suspect that few people would choose to write so candidly for public consumption and scrutiny about times that were so unimaginably filled with despair it was almost impossible to consider completing even the simplest of daily tasks, let alone being responsible for the care of my daughters and myself.

It has never been my intention to scare anyone when speaking of my darkest times, nor has it ever been my intention to be perceived as self-serving. But I do want to make it very clear to everyone—I am in a position where I am strong enough to openly share this story. And to be even more clear, I want to reinforce the message that life *is* worth living…every day, even when memories make you physically feel the pain of loss and recollections of events that transpired at the end haunt you. It took me some time to learn this lesson, but the important thing is that I have learned it because of the place where life took me, or, as friends and family have said, the hand that was dealt me.

So why should I share so much with so many people? The answer for me is simple: It *is* possible to regain perspective following a loss of such magnitude and the grief that follows. It *is* possible to recover from dark feelings and thoughts so that they will no longer consume you.

During the period in which I was writing this book, I overcame a tremendous number of hurdles. In some instances, while I was writing, I was in the midst of a chaotic situation and struggling to find a solution. This fueled my energy and drove me to write more, because this is a story of hope after all, and I felt compelled to share it.

I lost track of the number of hours I spent in Starbucks first on legal pad, then typing on my laptop. I wanted to get my whole story on paper and openly record all the details of the 12 months I describe in this book.

I suspect there will always be stigma associated with mental health issues. As a result, many individuals will refrain from discussing their struggles with depression, anxiety, PTSD, or other mental health diagnoses. Whatever their reasons, the hesitancy to speak out is their decision. I have chosen to take a different path, because I believe my story can provide comfort and hope to those who are grappling with mental health illnesses, whether associated with grief from the loss of a loved one or from some other origin. I want to speak out not only to encourage those experiencing difficult times to seek appropriate help but also to assure them that they *can* emerge from their darkest hours renewed, whole and functional—even able to experience joy again.

Everyone has a Story to Tell—So Tell It

It was the first time that my young widows' support group had changed its Thursday meeting time from 1:30 p.m. to 11 a.m. to better accommodate the members who had children in school. It was right after the school year had started, and the two group facilitators felt that attendance would be better if it were held in the late morning.

The room had the furniture positioned in a circle so that everyone could see each other and speak to the entire group. I was the first one who arrived and took my usual seat on one of the couches, in the corner, facing the door. As the time neared to begin the group session, the room began to fill up with the eight people that I had come to view as my friends. We were all there to help and support each other—no judgements, no put downs. This was a safe place where we could all talk about anything, and everything remained confidential. In fact, we were all prohibited from disclosing any information that would identify anyone individually or as a member of this group.

As 11 a.m. rolled around, one of the group's facilitators, who was a widow herself (her husband died in the World Trade Center during the September 11ᵗʰ attacks), told us that a new woman would be joining us. As a part of the tradition of welcoming a new member to the group, we each had to tell **our story**, specifically who our spouses were, how they passed away, and how we found the support group.

We went around the room, and each of us told our story. I had become accustomed to retelling mine—how Jen collapsed at home due to sudden cardiac arrest, how she was transported to the hospital and remained on life support, and how she eventually passed away. I always told people that Jen "collapsed" at home, but that she died nineteen days later after her life support was removed. It was important for me to ensure that particular detail was always explained during my recounting of the story.

When each of us had taken our turn sharing our stories, the facilitator reiterated an important message: "It is important that you tell your stories over and over again. Tell it to as many people as you can, because it is important that everyone tries to understand what you have been through. It is what made you who you are today."

Every one of our stories is unique, each filled with our own type of pain, suffering, tragedy, loss and recovery. No two stories are the same. No one suffers more than someone else, and no one's pain is less or more hurtful than someone else's. The grief, and yes, even the hopelessness and darkness, are universal feelings each of us experiences—regardless of age, gender, socioeconomic status, geographic location, color and/or religion.

It is horrible to lose your spouse, your partner in life, your soulmate. What's more, the loss of a spouse and the grief that follows for young widows/widowers, especially those with children, has another layer of misery and sadness. There are children who now only have one parent in their lives. For me, I worry everyday about how I am doing as a parent and whether my daughters, Rossella and Giada, will be all right in this world without their mother. I never thought I would have to even conceive of the notion that I would be raising them as a single parent. But I am. As a few people told me throughout 2018, "Joe, you were handed a really bad deck of cards in life."

In the spring of 2018, I began to journal about how I was feeling. For someone who wrote nothing other than his master's thesis in graduate school, I wrote whenever I could and for several different reasons. At first, writing proved to be therapeutic. Then I began to write about the experiences I had and the challenges I faced as a young widower with two children and how my endurance during that time taught me significant life lessons.

I have retold the story of Jennifer's, passing more times than I would like, but that story is part of my life now. The old me died with my wife back in 2017. The new me wants to retell this story and share it with as many people as possible, because I believe it is a story worth telling over and over again to as many people as possible—and I do believe it is a story of hope for people who seek comfort upon finding themselves in similar situations. There are many young widows and widowers who believe they are in situations that seem to be unsurmountable and overwhelming. To all those individuals, I can truly say there is hope.

Beyond the chance of helping my fellow widows and widowers, there is also another reason for me writing this book and recounting all of the devastating things that have happened to me. Two reasons actually…my twin daughters, Rossella and Giada.

Their mother was someone who touched the lives of everyone she met. Honestly, there was not one person who was not ravaged and rocked by Jen's sudden passing. Like me, Jen's friends and family were shocked and saddened by her untimely death. We felt the world had gotten a little less beautiful, a little less happy, and that it would never be the same again. Not for any of us. My daughters' mother was a force here on earth, but they did not have a lot of time with her to truly see how Jen affected everyone. It is up to me to make sure there is evidence of that. This story is the evidence to which they can refer to see and understand how special their mother was to everyone in her life.

There is no right or wrong way for a widow/widower to handle their grief. As I frequently remark to others: "There is no manual to instruct an individual how to handle and cope with the loss of a spouse." Jokingly I add, "If there is a manual, please let me see it."

I repeat, everyone's story is different. No two stories are the same. That means too that the matter in which a widow/widower deals with the aftermath of a spouse's death is neither right nor wrong. My story is not the "instruction manual." Rather, its goal is to be a source of hope for those who believe they are alone with their grief. Much like an implausible situation in which an individual would be dropped off at the base of Mount Everest without any climbing gear and told that they had to climb to the mountain's summit, widows/widowers will be faced with unthinkable and seemingly impossible tasks. In spite of this, they can overcome and accomplish whatever they set their minds to undertake in life.

2

Jen and Me

Before I get to the story of what happened in 2017 and 2018, it is important to spend time explaining how Jen and I met and how we fell in love. This is to not only provide everyone with a backdrop to this story, but also to reiterate how her passing was and is such a devastating loss for me and our children. People have told me that they love our story and the way our relationship grew from a casual friendship to a loving relationship and how because of this transition, the way we were together for so many of our young adult years. On the one hand, talking about my relationship with Jen brings many wonderful memories to the surface, and I tell the part of the story about our first years together and our early married life with joy. But talking about these memories is also painful because I know that we will no longer be able to create memories.

Jen and I were freshman at Pocono Mountain High School back in the fall of 1996 when we first met. We were in the same classes together. I still had all of my hair (albeit it would not stay around too much longer), and befriended Jen early on. We had a close-knit group of friends, did school projects together and ate lunch together.

Just like any typical 9th grader in this situation, I developed a schoolboy crush on Jen. Jen had long, dark hair, and always wore these dresses that made her stand out to me. There was one in particular, a green and black flowered pattern dress, that was my favorite. Jen kept it because she knew I loved it. In fact, I have it stored away at my house to this day.

Along with my crush, I also had a tremendous amount of shyness which prevented me from asking her to be my girlfriend. We would finish out the school year as friends, signing each other's yearbooks, and occasionally writing letters to each other in the summer of 1997 (this was before email was used as the preferred mode of communication). The letters we wrote to each other were typical of the way 14-year-old kids write each other: "How was your summer going?" "What have you been doing?" Even though we attended the same regional high school, Jen and I lived about on opposite ends of our rural Pennsylvania county.

We did exchange phone numbers in our letters and toward the end of summer, when we spoke on the phone, she asked me to the local carnival in her town. I accepted her invitation, but with the understanding that we were going as friends. I even asked her if any other people were coming. Much to my surprise, I found out much later when we were dating that Jen was hoping that the carnival would act as a catalyst for bringing us together as a couple. Jen wound up inviting another friend to the carnival that night, but we still had a great time.

For the next two years, Jen and I did not have classes together, although we did see each other at assemblies and at lunch. We remained friends, but we did not see each other outside of school. Additionally, this was still prior to the wide use of cell phones. We could not text and did not have our own email accounts yet.

Finally, in our senior year, 1999-2000, we had classes together again, though not as many as during our freshman year. Still, that year, I felt like I got to know Jen even better, and our friendship really blossomed.

After graduation, Jen and I were hanging out together, but it began to feel different. One day we were out by a lake close to her house, enjoying the summer weather, when I kissed her for the first time. I remember thinking that being with Jen was downright euphoric. Holding her hand, talking with her, seeing her warmth and compassion for others evoked feelings I had never experienced before, and it was wonderful. I treasured every moment with her.

When we started our freshman year of college, I was commuting to Penn State's campus in Allentown, Pennsylvania, about one hour from my house, four days a week, and Jen was commuting to Marywood University in Scranton, Pennsylvania, about one hour from her house but in the opposite direction. We made it a point to try to talk to each other almost every day and see each other on the weekends.

As our first semester went on, we grew closer to each other, and then finally on December 21, 2000, we basically said to one another, "I think we are officially a couple."

By this time, email was becoming a more widely accepted means of communication, but I chose to hand write Jen love letters and notes and give them to her when I saw her. Watching her face light up with enjoyment...watching her blush when I told her how much I loved her thrilled me. I was never at a loss for words when I wrote to her. I usually filled pages of loose-leaf paper and used every inch of a card when I wrote about how much she meant to me. I never repeated anything to her from letter to letter with the exception of how I signed my name. I always ended each letter, note, or card with the closing *Forever loving you*, which expressed a feeling that will never change with me.

In the summer of 2001, I switched majors from meteorology to political science and transferred from Penn State to East Stroudsburg University, which was only twenty minutes from my house. A week after the semester started, the September 11th attacks occurred. Many Americans witnessed the horrific events that started with the first plane striking the World Trade Center's North Tower. I did not see what was occurring until after the first tower collapsed, because I was in my American Government class. I watched in disbelief as the second tower collapsed. Shortly after, East Stroudsburg canceled classes for the rest of the day, and I drove home.

When I got home, there was a call from Jen who had managed to get through the jammed-up phone system. She asked me if any of my family members were in Manhattan during the attacks, which they were not, and inquired if I wanted to attend a church service with her later that day. I said no, because I was not very religious. That was the first time, and not the last time, that I ever questioned my religious beliefs. How could all those innocent people die? How was that fair? And how could all those children lose parents suddenly? In retrospect, when I consider what happened in our family 16 years later, that thought was filled with irony.

Months turned into years, and my relationship with Jen grew as we developed a deeper appreciation and love for each other. Holidays were filled with wonderful memories, and we established our own traditions and anniversaries that marked important days in our lives. We celebrated December 21st annually, as the anniversary of us officially dating, thankful that our bond was solid and tenacious. We also made time for each other whenever we could, between college, work and our families.

In the spring of 2004, we both graduated and went on to pursue our Masters' degrees. Jen wanted to purse her Master's degree in social work at the University of Pennsylvania in Philadelphia and I wanted to obtain my Master's degree in political science at East Stroudsburg University. Jen chose to stay with a family friend in Bridgeport, Pennsylvania, and commute to school by train during the week. Her family was back in Wilkes-Barre, Pennsylvania, and she came home on weekends to visit them and me.

We both knew around this time that we wanted to continue building a life together, and one day in November 2004, I travelled into New York City and picked out an engagement ring. I recall that I wanted to get out of the city as quickly as possible because I did not want to drop it or get mugged.

Already, I had begun to plan how I was going to ask Jen to marry me. I had purchased a small trinket box in the shape of a ring box. I knew that I wanted to pop the question to her before the end of the year. I picked a Saturday in December to go up to her house after work to propose to her. My plan was to do a fake proposal using the trinket box, and in the box have a note saying that I hoped her expression was just like this when I gave her the real ring. Then, I would IMMEDIATELY propose to her for real. I knew I was going to catch some serious hell for about two minutes. I also knew it would be worth it.

That night, I drove to Jen's house and at the bottom of the steps to her house, I proposed with the trinket box. Of course, she was excited at first, but when she discovered it was not for real, she flipped out. As I calmed her down, I asked her to help me into her house with bags from the trunk. When I opened the trunk, the real ring was lying on top of pillows. I got down on one knee. She said, "You're lucky you proposed to me right now." The date was December 11th, 2004. Exactly thirteen years later, to the day, Jen would take her last breath in hospice care, and leave me forever.

We set a wedding date for October 2006. We knew that we had to save money and plan things accordingly. Plus, Jen wanted to get her fill of reality wedding shows like Bridezillas (She was hardly a Bridezilla!).

We both finished graduate school. I struggled to find a job that was in line with my major, but Jen landed a job right away at a treatment center. While I conducted a job search, I worked odd jobs so we had money coming in for our wedding.

Jen's parents decided to move from Wilkes-Barre to Cincinnati, Ohio, in 2006, as Jen's father landed an excellent job as a machine adjuster. Jen and I agreed that she would move in with my parents and me so that we could continue to save money for our wedding. This was the first time Jen and I would be living together.

Meanwhile, my job search was not going well and I (we) was (were) feeling financial pressure. We decided to change things up, move to Cincinnati to temporarily live with Jen's parents, so that we could save money faster for our wedding. I was hoping that moving to a city like Cincinnati would better position me to land a job that would put me on a career track.

By the end of summer 2006, we were settled in with her parents, knowing that we would move back to Pennsylvania before our wedding that was now scheduled to take place in October 2007. Jen, of course, landed a job almost immediately, at a children's treatment center in Covington, Kentucky, right across the Ohio River, while I found a temporary job at a behavioral healthcare center's Human Resources Department. I continued to stay at the temporary job for several months until I landed a permanent position as a housing case manager at one of their satellite centers. Through both the temporary job and the permanent position I gained knowledge that proved valuable for my career later in life, and Jen was able to collect the hours that were required in order for her to apply for her and Licensed Social

Worker (LSW) and Licensed Clinical Social Worker (LCSW) credentials.

While we were in Cincinnati, we made trips back to Pennsylvania and continued to make plans for our wedding and find the apartment where we would officially start our life together. Jen's old company in Wilkes-Barre wholeheartedly wanted her back to their facility, now as a supervisor. This helped make our transition easier.

We moved to Kingston, Pennsylvania, in August 2007, and found a one-bedroom apartment with a huge balcony and a community pool. Jen and I loved the apartment because we finally felt that all of our hard work had paid off.

Between settling into our new apartment and with the wedding quickly approaching, Jen and I were busy. We had made all of the preparations we could for our wedding with the funds we had available, but we splurged and booked a ten-day honeymoon to Aruba. Everything was falling into place in the days leading up to the wedding. This was one of the happiest times of our lives.

Our wedding day was dry, no hint of rain, and was the only day that week that actually felt like fall (all of the other days that week had summer-like temperatures). A lot of people had told us that your wedding day would be over "in a blink of an eye," and they were absolutely correct. The entire day, as long and eventful as it was, went by very quickly for the two of us. We did not even eat at the reception, as we were too busy with the guests and festivities.

We left for our honeymoon three days later, which

was the best ten days we could have possibly had. It was especially wonderful because it was the first time we had travelled outside the country. We also actually managed to rest and relax together for more than just a couple of hours.

The months and years that followed our wedding were nice for us as a young married couple. We loved living in our apartment and were thankful that we had our health, family, and friends, but we continued to struggle financially. We routinely charged our groceries to a credit card, but we at least managed to pay our rent and our bills.

In 2008, I was hired to work full time as a supervisor at the treatment center at which Jen worked. I loved working with those kids, because I managed to act as a role model for them in their time of need. I believed that I did some good not only for the kids, but also for the staff as well. Comradery was strong among the staff, and as a team, we handled the challenges that were presented to us.

Then in the spring of 2009, new management took over the company. I was demoted as a result of restructuring and received a significant pay cut. I was reassigned to oversee the overnight staff members rather than continuing in my role managing the majority of the staff at the center. Within a couple of days of assuming my new role, Jen and I concluded that we did not want to continue living in Pennsylvania. My parents had moved to Monmouth County, New Jersey, the year prior, and we said: "We want to give Jersey a try."

Within six weeks of making the decision to relocate to New Jersey, I interviewed and was hired for a company based in Newark. I had provided my employer with only a week's notice of my intent to leave, and Jen had set a deadline to give her notice and leave. We placed most of our belongings in storage and temporarily moved in with my parents while we looked for a new apartment.

We only lived with my parents for a few months, but during that time we literally lived out of a suitcase because my parents' closets were full. The space was cramped, but we made things work. It paid off. In November 2009, we found a great apartment in Neptune, New Jersey, and made it our home for the next four years. In those four years a lot happened to Jen and me. We adjusted to living only ten minutes from the beach (although that adjustment was not hard at all), adopted a rescue cat, Anastasia, went on to further stabilize our finances by getting better paying jobs, but most importantly went from a family of two to a family of four in 2013 when Jen gave birth to our daughters.

The girls were born on August 17th, a Saturday. Jen woke up that morning, 37 weeks pregnant, having pains in her abdomen. I called her doctor, and his exact words, in a heavy Israeli accent were: "You need to get to the hospital. Your children are being born today." One hour later, after speeding up the Garden State Parkway and through the streets of Long Branch, Jen was admitted to the operating room where she had an emergency c-section. Both of the girls were born healthy, and Jen and the girls remained in the hospital for five days.

We remained in the apartment until the lease ran out in November 2013. It was cramped and tight living, but we loved it and made it work. Jen and I were thankful for every minute that we had together with the girls in the apartment, but we knew that we had to move to a bigger home.

We rented a townhouse in Tinton Falls, a neighboring town. From the moment Jen and I pulled up with the moving truck, we realized we had made a mistake. We knew the townhouse was not the ideal rental and had seen that it was in need of dire repairs when we looked at it with the realtor. But on moving day, when we saw that none of the repairs we had requested had been done, we got the message that our landlords were not the most reputable and reliable people. This sent us into a tailspin, and we acknowledged we had made the biggest blunder of our marriage and for our girls.

Jen and I both vowed that from that point on and for the rest of our lives we were never going to allow anyone to take advantage of us again—or allow our vulnerability in the face of challenges let us succumb to a situation like the one we found ourselves in at that time. We had both become stronger people as a result of our predicament, but Jen especially exuded confidence and credibility. She demanded respect and would not tolerate anyone standing in the way of her getting what she wanted or anything that she felt that she deserved in life. She truly took a stand against anything or anyone that was a threat to her or our well-being. Up until the day that Jen's heart stopped beating, I not only loved Jen but also saw her transform into a person whom I admired and respected and wanted to emulate.

As important, our renting the townhouse in Tinton Falls pushed us to do one more thing: buy our own house. We buckled down, like we did when we saved for our wedding. We tried to save every penny we could to put together a down payment on a house. We did it before, and we were going to do it again.

By the summer of 2014, we had saved what we thought was enough for the necessary down payment. Through the support group that Jen joined geared especially for mothers of twins, triplets, etc., we contacted a realtor, and began the search for our new home.

We narrowed our search to an area of Howell named Ramtown, in Monmouth County. Before too long we walked into a house and knew it was the one. We quickly put in an offer, and it was accepted. It had taken us over a decade to get to this point, but we were going to do it—settle into a house, raise children, and enjoy our lives together. We closed on July 29th, 2014 and moved into our new home one month later. We both knew that because of all of our hard work, patience, drive for success, and most importantly, our commitment to one another, that we had secured what we most desired in life.

We had all the material things in life that we yearned for throughout the years—a newly furnished home, two cars and careers that we both enjoyed. Still, there was one thing that Jen and I never forgot throughout the years— that our relationship and the fidelity we shared with each other was never going to change. It was a force, an energy. It was unshakable, priceless, and was never going to end. Equally as important, the incredible responsibility of raising two children further strengthened that bond. Giada and Rossella were our legacy.

Throughout all of the struggles, challenges and

downright crappy moments we have shared together, I know now that indeed those were the times that I cherish and miss the most. Those were the times I relied on Jen the most, looked to Jen for the support the most, and solidified the foundation that we had built together.

In retrospect, I look at those hard times as opportunities that allowed us to reaffirm our commitment to each other. The happy times were a result of those most difficult times. They were the times in which we experienced the most growth, and I have gratitude for having grown through them with Jen.

3

How Are You Doing?

"How are you doing?" For me, these are the four most dreaded words that will come up in any conversation. Most of the time I truly did not how to answer that question since that day in November 2017.

"How do you think I am doing?" I wanted to say. I got asked the question so many times that it made me angry.

As someone who lost his wife suddenly, that question is something that should be fairly easy to answer: "I am feeling lousy. I am feeling angry. I am feeling depressed."

Even worse, once people did indeed ask the question, they would follow up with: "As good as you can be, I guess."

I would then say to myself: "Well, why ask that question in the first place?"

For months after Jen passed away, I would cringe when those four words came up in conversation. I would force myself to allow people, mostly my friends and family, to ask me that question, and I made sure that I would have a somewhat normal response. But really, was there any normal to my situation?

Though this question prompted my anger and annoyance, I slowly began to realize my friends and family were asking because they truly cared about my four-year-old daughters and me. Actually, this was my absolute, first realization that I had a support network and was not going to be alone, because, when Jen passed away, I wholeheartedly felt that that no one was going to be there for me—that I would always be alone. When I say alone, I mean I feared that emotionally no one was going to care how I was feeling as I coped with the loss of my wife of ten years. I eventually learned that this was not the case.

How are you doing? In the months following Jen's untimely passing those words were indeed asked time and time again. Eventually, I realized most people were not trying to pry and that in the time of a tremendous tragedy, people overlook most petty differences and focus on the person in need.

Soon, then, these four dreaded words, "How are you doing?" turned into words of comfort. I did hear them whenever I met up with my friends or went to professional or family functions. Soon, hearing those words told me that each person sincerely wanted to know if they could help Giada, Rossella and me.

Actually, right after Jen died, my dear friend, Dennis, told me that I had to let people help me…had to allow them the chance to do whatever they felt they could to assist and support me in my time of need. For almost my entire life, I greatly disliked allowing others to help me. It made me believe that I was not capable of coping with difficult situations on my own. I always believed that I was more than capable to handle any challenge on my myself. Jen and I consistently worked hard for what we had earned in life. But when Jen fell ill and especially right after she died, I was an individual whose life had completely collapsed. So, I began to ask myself if letting people into my life to help me…if their acts of kindness that typically began with those four little words, "How are you doing?" was so terrible after all?

Changing my outlook enabled me to take the first steps towards healing. This is when I first noticed that the depth and immediacy of the pain and suffering would not remain, and that change, though small, would be possible, as long as I let people and change itself to enter my life.

Dennis, in particular, became an integral part of my journey through recovery, and yes, widows are consistently in a journey toward recovery. Dennis was the one who repeatedly said to me: "Joe, you are in recovery." He reminded me of this over and over again, but it did not resonate with me until one night in the winter of 2018, when I was on the phone with him, and he equated my situation to an individual who is recovering from dependence on drugs and alcohol.

This analogy was part of a language that I understood. Dennis and I worked together at two residential detox centers. He was the executive director, and I was employed as a compliance director, tasked with managing the licensing process for each facility's respective state regulatory agencies.

I witnessed Dennis transform a group of individuals

into a cohesive team that truly worked well together. Employees that worked in the Massachusetts facilities he managed, as well as individuals who sought treatment, looked to Dennis for his leadership, knowledge, and inspiration. Following Jen's death, Dennis become one of my greatest friends, and a de facto family member. As important, Jen had met him a couple of times, and immediately saw that he was genuine, authentic and a loyal friend.

Dennis, who lives in the Berkshires about four hours north of my Jersey Shore home, and I were more than just colleagues. In 2016, we opened up a facility together in Northeastern Massachusetts. Soon thereafter, in the summer of 2016, Dennis decided to return to his former employer in Northwest Connecticut so that his days of traveling the three-hour trek up and down the Massachusetts Turnpike were done. I admit now that I did not want to see Dennis leave our mutual employer, but it made sense. His wife and Great Danes missed him, and he had a chronically ill brother who lived near his home town.

So, Dennis left, and I stayed. But Dennis knew how unhappy I was with my current situation. Still, he repeatedly told me: "Be patient" and "Things will fall into place." He also vigorously campaigned to have me join him. I envisioned me working remotely from New Jersey and he would work in Connecticut.

I knew Dennis was looking out for my best interests. He was and still is a person I relied upon for guidance and support. I trusted him and knew he would never steer me wrong. Also, of significance: this was the first time I learned that sometimes I really did not have any control of a situation. I just had to believe that events occurred at a particular time, in a particular order, for a particular reason.

Weeks turned into months, but I finally received a much-needed phone call from the woman who would eventually become my next boss, asking if I would be interested in "switching teams." Six weeks later, I found myself on 9th Avenue in New York City, interviewing with the two primary owners of Dennis's company. I remember that I could barely eat my hamburger when we went out to lunch, not wanting to spill anything on my suit.

After my lunch interview, I remember calling Jen from the parking lot of the Frank Lautenberg train station in Secaucus, New Jersey where I had parked my car to take the seven-minute train ride into New York's Penn Station. (I hated driving into Manhattan when I did not have to, especially when I had to attempt to find parking). I told Jen that I was shocked that it went so well, and that a company as high-profile as this was interested in someone like me. As always, Jen reassured me that I was great at what I did. Her words of confidence stick with me to this day. Even after her death, Jen's words of support, confidence, and love have been planted in my soul and can never be taken away.

I also called Dennis once I got onto the New Jersey Turnpike and headed south. I was still in shock that I had just met with the owners of a multi-million-dollar company and that they were very much impressed with me.

All that Dennis kept saying to me was: "Joe, why are

you surprised? Look at what you have done in your life."
I allowed that to sink in. Both Jen and Dennis have had a
profound impact on how I regard myself professionally.

Two weeks after the interview in New York, and a
trip to Northwest Connecticut for a second round of
interviews, an employment letter came in the mail. As
the newest employee of Dennis's company, my primary
responsibility was to assist with the opening of two new
treatment facilities. One was going to be right in the
heart of downtown Manhattan.

Before making this move, I was the type of person
that needed to live a structured, scheduled life. I always
had to have control over as much as I possibly could
because that provided me stability that in turn gave me
comfort. If there were any deviations, I was heading
for trouble. As I came to realize those six-plus months
between Dennis leaving the facility in Northeastern
Massachusetts and me joining him served as a test for
me in how well I could manage the uncertainty of life
and events being beyond my control. In fact, this was
the first time I understood that sometimes there would
be nothing I could do to help navigate the happenings
in my life. Certain situations *were* completely out of
my control. That was a fact I had to accept. And, so, I
learned to trust things were "just going to work out" *and*
that I had to learn to live one day at a time. Sometimes
even one hour at a time. Ironically, this would become
even clearer based on the events that transpired in the
months that followed.

4

Nineteen Days

In a little under three weeks, my life changed completely. The transformation was so incredibly painful, so incredibly traumatic and the likes of which most people never endure in their entire lives—most certainly not one month before their 35th birthday. I am able to recall the details of those 19 days because of their magnitude.

It all began in November of 2017. It was about a week before Thanksgiving, and Jen and I had just put up our Christmas decorations. We had agreed in years past that it was much easier to fully decorate the house for the holidays during a school day so that we could get everything done more quickly, and then surprise Giada and Rossella when they got home from daycare. We would decorate the entire house and put up four Christmas trees: one in the dining room, one in the family room where our stockings hung over the fireplace, one in our daughters' bedroom and the final one in the living room at the front of our house.

Jen beautifully decorated the house every year before

Thanksgiving, and this holiday season was no different. Santas, snowmen, and reindeer would overtake the house every November and December. I always made sure the exterior of our house had plenty of lights, and I would tightly wind strands of white lights around our Japanese maple tree. I aspired to have the house look as close as possible to Clark Griswald's house in "National Lampoon's Christmas Vacation".

Our holiday preparations were progressing on schedule. Wednesday, November 22nd, the day before Thanksgiving, Jen went off to work as usual, and I was working from home. I had the benefit of working from home four days a week and traveling by bus to New York City one day a week. Just that week, I had switched my city day to Monday from Wednesday. As it turned out, I am very thankful I did.

Jen and I were geared up and excited for the upcoming holiday season. We were planning to go to my sister's house in Pennsylvania for Thanksgiving dinner. The day after Thanksgiving, Black Friday, Jen planned on following her usual custom of shopping throughout the night and into the wee hours of the morning. That Saturday, we had planned on taking our daughters on a Polar Express ride in Phillipsburg, New Jersey, a popular holiday pastime for kids in New Jersey.

Jen and I planned to jumpstart the Thanksgiving weekend festivities with a movie date Wednesday afternoon. Jen was a big Mark Wahlberg fan, and I was a big Will Ferrell fan, so the recently released *Daddy's Home 2* was the perfect choice.

Jen and I agreed that we would see the 2 p.m. show

at the movie theater across the street from the kids' daycare, pick up the girls, and then go home and prepare the food we would bring to Thanksgiving dinner.

The movie was not only funny, but also, I remember holding Jen's hand throughout almost the entire film, letting it let go only when my hand got sweaty. We laughed, snuggled together in the reclining leather seats, and really enjoyed the break from work, the girls, and all of our other troubles (Now I wish that I had those troubles back in my life). My time that day with Jen is something that I will always cherish and hold close to my heart for the rest of my life.

When the movie was over, Jen left to pick up Giada and Rossella from daycare, and I went straight home to get a head start on blowing the leaves off of our front lawn. Jen came home while I was doing this, brought the girls inside and made a beeline for the kitchen.

When I accomplished what I could with the leaves, I eventually made my way inside, and found Jen working away in the kitchen. The girls were in the living room watching one of their favorite Netflix shows, "High Five," a syndicated Australian kids' show with performers singing and dancing.

I had walked into the kitchen through the dining room so that I would not disturb Jen with her meal preparations. To this day, I do not remember how the conversation started, but I remember saying to her: "If I did not have bad luck, I would have no luck at all."

Jen replied, "You have great luck." I do recall how the conversation ended—me kissing the back of her neck. Then I walked out of the kitchen.

I returned to the living room and settled in with the girls who were zoned into their television show. I was admiring the work Jen and I did with the Christmas decorations just five days earlier, when I then heard the **WORST** sound in my life. It was a noise that will forever haunt me. Jen called out, "Joseph." This was followed by a loud thump.

When I walked into the kitchen, there was Jen, the woman I loved most in the world, lying on the floor, unconscious and convulsing, foaming from her mouth. I tapped her a couple of times on her shoulder, frantically called out her name, then realized that she was in trouble, and needed medical assistance.

I ran to the cordless phone in our living room, passed the girls and told them to stay out of the kitchen. I called 911 while Jen continued to shake uncontrollably.

I remembered that when you call 911, you have to remain calm and make sure that you tell the operator everything clearly, because any delay in relaying the correct information to the dispatcher could be troublesome for the victim. I recall telling the operator that Jen was on the floor, seizing and shaking almost violently. I had placed the phone on the kitchen counter above us. Jen would not stop convulsing, and when I told this to the 911 dispatcher, he instructed me to place Jen on her side so that she did not choke on her tongue. A few seconds went by and it clicked with me what was really happening. Jen was potentially dying in front of me.

The girls stood in the kitchen door frame and were asking me: "Is Mommy ok? Is Mommy dead?" I thought to myself, how would my daughters even know to ask me that? How did they even know what it means to die? In a split moment, and not in my best judgment, I lied to them and said that Mommy dropped a pot on her foot.

I did my best to remain calm as I realized that these could be Jen's final moments alive. I managed to get the girls back into the living room. Minutes felt like years. In the background, I could hear the approaching sirens as Jen's labored breathing turned into gasps. She was wearing one her favorite black shirts that was the same color as her hair. I was doing my best to keep Jen on her side, and then I remembered that I had to go unlock and open the front door so that the paramedics could get in.

I went right back to holding Jen on her side, facing me so that I could watch her. Her eyes were closed, and her gasps were now silenced, but there was still saliva rolling down her mouth onto the floor. I had to keep talking so that I knew the operator was on the phone with me.

By the time the first paramedics—two volunteer first aid responders from Ramtown, the section of Howell in which we lived—six minutes had elapsed. The EMT's quickly came up the stairs from the front door. As soon as they got into the kitchen, they immediately began pulling out their emergency medical equipment so that they could keep Jen alive. I got out of their way and realized that I had to get Giada and Rossella out of the house right then.

I ran out the front door and feverishly waved to our friends, Josh and Nicole, who lived right across the street from us. Their daughter, Lily, who is thirteen months younger than Giada and Rossella, was my girls' best friend. In fact, Josh, Nicole and Lily had become our closest friends, and we had begun to regard them as family. From her living room window, Nicole saw me flagging her down from my front steps, asking her to hurry over to my house. I ran back inside, grabbed the girls' sneakers from their bedroom closet, and literally swooped them up into my arms and handed them over to Nicole who by now was at my front door. All I remember saying to Nicole was, "Please take them." Giada and Rossella did not even have time to put their sneakers on their feet. I knew they had to get out of the house.

As soon as the girls were safely with Nicole, I went back into the house, and saw what seemed to be close to ten people in my kitchen, working on Jen. Medical equipment was everywhere. My kitchen table was shoved out of the way so the paramedics could kneel and work over Jen. I asked the first responders if she was going to be all right, but did not get a yes or no.

Police officers and paramedics then bombarded me with questions. "Does she take any medications? What was she doing today? Is she allergic to anything? Was she complaining of pain?"

I did my best to answer. "Yes, for her thyroid and birth control. No. No, she just called out my name and I heard a loud thump."

One of the Howell police officers asked me, "What is her social security number?" I told him right away to his surprise.

At one point, it occurred to me that this was going to be the end. I was going to be a widower. I started pleading and repeating, "I cannot be a widower."

I remember someone yelling out "We have a pulse,"

and then feeling some relief. Jen was going to make it. She was not going to leave me and our girls.

Foolishly, I then asked one of the EMT's if she was going to go to the hospital. "Absolutely," he said. "We are prepping her now for transport to Ocean Medical Center."

Thoughts then immediately ran through my head. *I have to check on the girls at Josh and Nicole's to make sure they are okay, I have to call Jen's parents right away* (They were on their way to Pennsylvania from Virginia for Thanksgiving at Jen's brother's house) and *I better grab both Jen's cell phone and my cell phone with a cell phone charger because I will now need to communicate with lots of people.*

I first went to Josh and Nicole's house; the girls were playing with Lily and cleverly Josh and Nicole kept the three girls away from the windows so that they could not see anything that was going on at my house. I told them what had happened, and that Jen was going to the hospital. The girls saw me and asked me if Mommy was okay. All I could say was that she was getting the help she needed.

I ran back across the street to my house, grabbed both cell phones, and called Jen's mom, who had just crossed into Pennsylvania from Maryland. I told her that she had to get to New Jersey right away. Fortunately, my in-laws were on the Pennsylvania Turnpike, so they were only a couple of hours away from our house. I also called Jen's brother, Emad, and without hesitation he said that he was on his way too. He had about a three-hour trip ahead of him.

The paramedics and police officers were finally

preparing to move Jen to the ambulance. I ran back to Josh and Nicole's one more time and asked them if they could make sure that all of the utilities and the Christmas lights were properly shut off. The paramedics were going to leave any minute, and I could not afford to do anything that would prevent Jen from being transported to the hospital. I also asked Josh and Nicole if they would be able to keep the girls at their house, because I did not know when Jen's family would arrive. They already had the presence of mind to ask Giada and Rossella to sleepover. I was thankful they were thinking so quickly on their feet.

I told the girls: "I love you. Daddy is going to go with Mommy." I hugged Josh and Nicole and ran back to our house. More neighbors had gathered on their front lawns to see what was happening.

The paramedics began to move Jen out of the house. They did not place her on a typical stretcher that had legs and wheels. Rather, they placed her in a stretcher that was black and almost looked like a blanket with handles on all sides so that she could be carried easily down the stairs to the ambulance. I stood and watched in disbelief that this was how they were bringing my wife out of the house. Little did I know that this was the last time we would be in our house together as husband and wife.

The ambulance ride to the hospital seemed to take an eternity, yet it was only four miles from our house. During the trip, the driver informed me that he would be driving rather slowly so that the EMTs' movements would be steady as they continued to work on Jen.

They had stabilized her. Jen's heart rate was back, and she was alive, but they were pumping air into her lungs using an ambu bag. The EMT's kept trying to talk to Jen, asking her to "stay with them." Every minute or so, I would talk to Jen from the front seat, telling her to breathe, stay with me, and that Giada and Rossella were fine. I knew that if she were conscious, she would have wanted to know that the girls were okay.

The ambulance finally arrived at the hospital. I jumped out and ran to the back so that I could be next to Jen when the EMTs wheeled her out. They had to wait a few minutes before they carried her out of the ambulance, because they wanted to make sure she was bundled up properly for the cold November air. Once they secured her, they brought her into the nearest triage room in the ER.

It was amazing to see how many people ran to Jen's assistance when they situated her in her hospital room. By that time, I had spoken to Jen's parents twice. They were unfortunately stuck in traffic outside Philadelphia. Within the first thirty minutes of our arrival, I also spoke to my father and sister, both in Pennsylvania; Jen's boss, Kim; Jen's best friend, Pam, who was up in Buffalo, New York, visiting her in-laws for the holiday. I also left a message with Dennis, as I was scared and needed his guidance and support.

I sat on a lone, blue vinyl chair right outside Jen's hospital room, replaying our day and trying to figure out what had happened to her. *We were at the movies, snuggling and holding hands. She went to pick up the girls and came home and started cooking while I raked leaves. We exchanged a few words in the kitchen and I kissed the back of her neck. Then out of nowhere, everything changed.*

In real time, I watched as countless staff members went in and out of Jen's room as they worked to stabilize her. I also had the chance to thank the EMT who kept air flowing into Jen's lungs in the ambulance.

A couple of times, I managed to pop my head into Jen's room while the nurses and doctors were attending to her, and all I could see were a never-ending amount of tubes, wires, and hospital equipment. Somewhere underneath all that equipment and emergency gear, my wife—the woman I vowed to love, honor, and cherish, was fighting for her life. This was the first time I experienced the feeling that I had not protected her. It was a sentiment that I never felt before, and it made me feel absolutely horrible. How could this have happened? How could my wife with whom I'd been on a date a few hours earlier, end up on life support? The questions started to pile up in my mind and little did I know it was going to take an extremely long and painstaking time for those answers to come to me.

As the minutes and hours passed, hospital personnel approached me, asking me what seemed to be dozens of questions: "Did your wife take drugs? What medications was she on? What did she tell you today?"

I tried to remain calm, but instead I became irritated, because I felt no one was giving me any answers. "My wife just collapsed in the kitchen" was what I repeated. *My wife did not do anything wrong; she did not deserve any of this. Just tell me what happened, and that she is going to be fine.* That was all I wanted to say to them.

My father's friend Sandy showed up at the hospital, seemingly out of nowhere. Sandy lived locally, and he informed me that my dad had called him, told him what had happened, and asked him to stay with me at the hospital. All I could do was recount the sudden, horrible events of the day. Sandy was as shocked as everyone else to whom I told this story: A 35-year old woman, who exercised, ate healthy, and took every precaution to take care of herself, just ended up in the hospital from apparently from sudden cardiac arrest. How does something like that happen out of nowhere?

Sandy tried to make me feel better, but I was in shock, and his comforting did little to help. At this point, Sandy called my father and described me as being "in shock but fine" (which was a pretty funny way of characterizing me because I really was not fine). I told Sandy that there was nothing he could really do for me and said that he could leave and go home, but I appreciated him coming to the hospital. He asked me if I was sure if I was going to be okay, and I told him that Jen's family would soon be arriving. So, he left, but told me that if I needed him to come back, he would return as quickly as he could.

I was alone for about another hour or so. Then Jen's parents arrived, and Jen's brother came in right after them. All three of them immediately asked me if I had heard anything from the doctors. They wanted answers about what went wrong and how this could have happened to someone who was so healthy? Jen's father frantically asked me what she ate that day, thinking that maybe someone did something to her food.

All four of us were taking turns, crying, consoling each other, fearing that the worst was going to happen. We all also took turns going into Jen's room, drawing the curtain back, and standing there in disbelief that Jen was breathing on a respirator and fighting to stay alive.

A few doctors periodically joined us. I kept hearing them say the word *virus* and identify *virus* as the likely cause of Jen's condition. But weren't viruses something that came and went in 24 to 48 hours, and here was Jen on life support? They did tell us, however, that Jen suffered from sudden cardiac arrest. Clinically, she had died at the house.

How could this have happened to someone so young. So healthy. So vital? I replayed the last few days and kept asking myself how Jen had felt last week, yesterday and in the days, hours and minutes leading up to that night. There were moments she had felt tired or had not felt like eating a big meal, but none of this was abnormal. Jen and I had four-year old twin daughters. Fatigue was part of parenting. We had gotten certainly enough sleep that week and there were no "red flags" that would have made me even consider thinking that Jen's heart would suddenly stop.

It was sometime after 8pm that the four of us realized that we had not eaten anything for dinner. Jen's brother offered to go and get pizza from a nearby Domino's. We all liked pizza, but that night, eating was not something to enjoy. We just needed to eat because we were tired and hungry and needed fuel, because we had no idea how long it would be until Jen was moved up to the critical care unit, the CCU. Meanwhile, I again called Nicole to check on the girls. They were asleep, she said, and thankfully not too scared about what they had seen.

The four of us ate our dinner in one of the waiting rooms down the hall from Jen's room. We all barely ate our pizza. We felt that this was some type of dream, a nightmare really; something that we all hallucinated, and we wanted to wake up from it. Unfortunately, waking up from a bad dream was not our reality.

It was after we finished our pizza that one of the emergency room doctors told us that Jen was going to be moved up to the CCU, but he had no idea what time the room would be available for her. The doctor told me "she will probably be in the hospital for a week or so, but she would get to go home." All of her vitals had stabilized except for her breathing—she was breathing solely with the help of the respirator. I did not care what help Jen needed; I just wanted her to come home where she belonged with our daughters and me.

The wait was painstaking, but around midnight she was finally moved up from the triage room in the ER to her suite in the CCU. I remember there was literally a team of nurses and technicians that moved Jen's bed up to the sixth floor at Ocean Medical Center. I can still recall how her breathing was heavy, and that nurses kept telling me that she was not taking any breaths on her own.

At first, we were not allowed in Jen's CCU room. We were instructed to stay in the waiting room outside the CCU's main entrance. There were about fifteen cushioned seats scattered around the room, and one flat screen TV that was affixed to the wall in the corner of the waiting room. The hospital staff provided coffee and individually wrapped muffins to the people who sat in the waiting room.

Once Jen was situated in her suite, Jen's parents decided to go back to our house. Jen's brother and I decided to stay at the hospital as long as we could. We were prepared to sleep in the waiting room if we had to, even though there were no beds or lounge chairs that would allow us to stretch out. Because it was so late, we decided that we were going to let Giada and Rossella sleep at Josh and Nicole's house for the night and get them in the morning.

After Jen's parents left the hospital, Jen's brother and I tried our best to occupy the time, but nothing eased our anxiety. We wanted to see Jen, but we had no choice but to wait until we received permission from the hospital staff to do so.

It was sometime after 12:30 a.m. when the CCU staff informed Emad and I that we were allowed to go into Jen's suite. We had to be escorted because the doors into the CCU were operated by a badge swipe system.

Walking down the hallway to her room, I once again became filled with the fear that this was not going to end well—that Jen was not going to make it. I walked into her suite and someone could have knocked me over with a feather. Jen was in dire straits. There were still nurses getting her properly situated, monitors beeping, lights flashing, and my emotions were going crazy. I felt scared, heartbroken, and in shock all at the same time. No one was able to provide us with any definitive answers as to why this happened. The only thing that the medical personnel were able to tell me was that her heart was beating very slowly and irregularly. More tests were needed, but the cause of her condition remained a large mystery.

Emad and I were only allowed to stay in Jen's room for a little while. We were told that she was placed in "therapeutic hypothermia," which meant that she would be comatose for 48-72 hours. For 24-36 hours, her body temperature would be lowered. Then, her body temperature would be raised for 24-36 hours. This was done to stave off any possible damage to her brain or organs. There was no way for her to acknowledge that we were in the room, no means for her to communicate with any of the hospital staff, her brother, or me. Her eyes were closed, and she was not moving at all, not even the slightest twitch or reflex. She was receiving a constant flow of medications through IV's, one for pain, one to fight any possible infections, and most importantly one to keep her in a sedated state.

Whenever I had the chance, I held Jen's hand, even though it was enmeshed with wires and tubes. Her hands, even though they were as cold as that November night, still had plenty of the warmth and love that we had built over the last 17 years as a couple.

It was around 1 a.m. when Emad and I decided that it was better to go home and try to get some sleep. The nurses and on-call doctors reiterated that because of the therapeutic hypothermia, there was no way of determining how much, if any, brain damage Jen had endured as a result of her collapse. This would prove to be a true test in patience for me as I waited days to see if Jen would need more intense medical treatment or physical therapy or at the very least figure out when she could see the girls again. But in reality, whether I realized it or not, I was already adopting a widower's mindset— learning how to manage my feelings when time and life itself just seems to stop as I waited for any type of hope and comfort.

I did not have my car at the hospital, so I had to ride home with Emad. The roads were deserted. It was now technically Thanksgiving, which was ironic because none of us had nothing to be thankful for. When we arrived home, Jen's parents were still up waiting for our update. Jen's mother said that she had gone to the supermarket and purchased a small turkey and other sides for a Thanksgiving dinner, even though none of us wanted to celebrate the holiday. I then excused myself for the night, knowing that I had to try and get some sleep.

As I lay in bed that night, I saw that half the bed was empty. Jen had left a pile of library books on her nightstand. I stared at the books and wondered if she was ever going to read them, then stared at the ceiling in the dark. Why this had happened to someone who loved life, nurtured her children and obeyed her doctors? How had Jen ended up suffering cardiac arrest in front of her family? I lay there in disbelief, trying to convince myself that maybe this was all some type of bad dream, and that I was going to wake up and have Jen next to me. How desperately I wanted that, but deep down knew that was not going to be the way things played out.

I am not sure how, but I did manage to get some sleep that night, probably out of sheer exhaustion. I woke up the next day, immediately shaved, dressed, and made my way down to the hospital while Jen's parents got the girls from Josh and Nicole's.

The CCU waiting room was empty that morning except for two men who were still there from the night before, waiting for news about their aunt who was gravely ill. I had notified the nurses' desk that I was outside in the waiting room. Family and friends kept calling to see how we were all holding up. Looking back, I do not know how I was able to talk to anyone, let alone be there for the girls in the days immediately following Jen's collapse.

I spent the majority of Thanksgiving Day in the hospital, sitting right beside Jen while Jen's parents, Emad, and his wife, Sara, took turns coming to the hospital and watching the girls at home. We did have dinner that night, though it was the last thing any of us wanted to do.

I talked to two doctors who were initially guarded when discussing Jen's prognosis, though one did tell me straight out that Jen might never recover. He said he wanted to make sure that I was fully aware of potential outcomes. The thought of not having Jen with me, fulfilling our dreams together, was scary as hell. I tried to put that out of my mind as best as I could and force myself to believe that people must have faith, even in the darkest of times, against insurmountable odds. For the entire time my wife was in the hospital, fighting for her life, I had to fight alongside her, because physically she was not capable of doing that for herself. My father, who is not a religious or spiritual man—especially since my mother died of cancer in 2012—told me that if you lose faith, you lose. Those words still resonate with me to this day and reinforced something my therapist said to me months later about me not giving up faith and hope during this frightening time: that it is not like to me to surrender and drown in despair.

The hospital had set times in which visitors were allowed into patient's rooms. There were two hours in the early afternoon, ninety minutes in the late afternoon, and one hour later in the evening. I tried my best to be by Jen's side as much as I could; sometimes I stayed past visiting hours, and the nurses were usually agreeable to me being in Jen's room.

For two days, I watched as Jen remained in her comatose state and patiently waited for someone to tell us any positive news, and for Jen to open her eyes and smile at me. Hours seemed to be years, and at home, the nights were long and I barely slept. And then there were the constant phone calls from friends and family asking how Jen was doing.

Saturday morning, November 25th, I received a phone call from the CCU nurse assigned to Jen. They were going to end her therapeutic hypothermia, take her off the Propofol, and try to see if there was any significant damage to her organs, including her brain. I sped through the streets of Brick Township to the hospital, thankfully there were no security guards at the front desk and in no time reached the CCU and the on-duty nurse who led me back to Jen. He had begun to awaken her to see if she would respond.

I immediately went to her bedside, squeezed her hand, and started talking to her, pouring my heart out to her, hoping that she would somehow, someway acknowledge me. I wanted her to know that I was at her side when she was in the greatest battle of her life. Her eyes were opening but they were not focusing on me when I spoke to her. Her pupils were rolling around from one side to another, back into her head. The nurse gave me a look that showed me that he knew this was not good. Still, I kept my faith, because I felt that I was not going to let any negativity hurt Jen in any way. She was showing some basic reflexes, she was taking some breathes on her own, coughing, and her legs did move somewhat on their own, but she was not responding as someone should when coming out of a sedated state.

Not long after, I experienced some of the absolute lowest moments in my life.

"Her chances are not good, and she will probably never recover," the doctor told us.

I started to breathe heavily and began to feel very lightheaded. Within a minute, I had dropped out of my chair, sprawled out on the floor, yelling that I was going to lose Jen. The doctor immediately paged to have a stretcher come up to the CCU waiting room to take me down to the emergency room. I could not control my breathing; it was becoming very rapid. I was hyperventilating. Next thing I remember was that I had four grown men place me on a stretcher and wheel me to the emergency room. I gave Jen's parents my wallet and cell phone and told them to call my father and sister.

I remember telling my admitting nurse that "I could not be a widower."

She said "Honey, I did not want to be one either, but I did, and you will make it."

I was placed on a heart monitor and given Ativan to calm me down. My in-laws came down to my room and told me that they had called my father and sister and that they were on their way to New Jersey. Emad came in the room and hugged me while I was lying in my hospital bed.

The Ativan started to do it job very effectively. I managed to fall asleep, for how long I still do not remember. I had to be awakened by a nurse. As soon as I was able to, I told the nurse that I wanted to go back upstairs to see Jen. The medication still had a strong effect on me, so when I was able to be discharged from the emergency room, I had to be brought up to Jen's CCU suite in a wheelchair. By then, my uncle, aunt, and cousins from Queens and Northern New Jersey were in the CCU waiting room and were taking turns visiting with Jen.

I was wheeled to Jen's bedside and took her hand and did not let go that entire time. Meanwhile, everyone kept asking me the questions that people had been asking me for the previous three days: "Was she sick? Did she complain about not feeling well?" Are the girls ok?"

They were very helpful, though, and advocated for me by asking questions about things that I just did not think of or was too scared to ask. They tried piecing together as much information as they could about what may have happened, but everyone still remained dumbfounded.

By late that afternoon, I was able to walk on my own, though I was still in shock over what the doctor had said that morning. My aunt convinced me to get a second opinion.

The following Monday morning, November 27th, I started calling other doctors from other hospitals in New Jersey, in hopes of finding someone who would give me more insight. I believed that there had to be something more that could be done for Jen. I was not fully convinced that Jen would die, but I knew it was a very real possibility. Everyone I spoke to kept telling me that I had to keep hope and faith alive, and I was compelled to do everything to help Jen in her time of need.

I was very surprised when I called one phone number and got a doctor on his personal cell phone at 7:30 a.m. on a Monday morning. I had never met him and did not know him before I spoke to him on the phone, but he listened to me as I recounted the events that had unfolded over the last few days and offered to review Jen's case with the doctor attending to her at the hospital. I was blown away by this man's kindness and generosity. He was a busy doctor who probably had dozens of patients, but he was willing to take the time to help another person who was in need. His kindness and humanity meant a great deal to me and I was soon to discover that I would see more and more of this.

Shortly after Jen was taken out of therapeutic

hypothermia, she began to suffer from uncontrollable seizures, some that even lasted for prolonged periods of time. The seizures were so incredibly severe that it was necessary to keep her sedated to prevent any potential brain damage. It broke my heart to see Jen like this and to know that if they tried to wake her up, it could possibly cause her further harm.

Jen did receive an EEG that day and in the meantime, I met with numerous doctors and repeatedly asked: "Is there something that Jersey Shore University Medical Center (a nearby trauma center) can be doing that Ocean Medical Center is not?"

All the doctors assured me they were doing everything they could for Jen." The neurologist on staff who was attending to Jen had ordered another EEG on Tuesday to assess her brain activity and determine if the seizures had continued. He was also one of the doctors who had given Jen the dismal prognosis. I spoke with him that Tuesday morning and confirmed that Jen was receiving an EKG that afternoon. Approximately one hour after her EKG was completed, Jen's nurse called me and said that the neurologist wanted to transport her to Jersey Shore so that she could have 24-hour EKG monitoring, and potentially control and stop the seizures. I was thrilled and gave my verbal consent to transport her. I went back to the hospital that night to visit Jen before they transported her, feeling some type of temporary relief that she was making headway towards recovery.

Her final night at Ocean Medical Center was the first time I started a ritual that I would continue to do for the remainder of Jen's time in the hospital. I would bring with me between five and seven letters or cards that I had written to Jen since the beginning of our relationship and read them to her. I thought that if she could hear me it would not only help her recover, but also make her feel better and comfort her. I also came to the conclusion, however, that if she could not hear me, at least I could say what I wanted to, in private, before any decisions would have to be made about removing her from life support.

I had also started a "texting campaign" to family and friends, sending nightly updates on Jen's condition. I wanted to make sure that every night everyone had the information, as best as I understood it from the doctors and nurses. I also told people how Giada and Rossella were doing, as well as what I was doing to help Jen recover, including telling everyone about our ritual.

There were many people who visited Jen in the hospital: her boss, her co-workers, her aunts, uncles, cousins, as well as my family and friends. Everyone who came to visit Jen was just like me—completely shocked, as well as overwhelmed with grief. Everyone held Jen's hand, spoke to her with hope, telling her that she had to get better so that she could do a favorite shared activity with them. When they were with me privately, though, it was evident that they were consumed by the situation. Whether or not they verbalized this, I could tell when I looked into their eyes.

The night Jen was transported to Jersey Shore was a big night for me because I thought the move could possibly be the beginning of the path towards recovery. She continued to have seizures, but now they were going to be able to monitor them around the clock.

Additionally, Jersey Shore permitted visitors to come at any time, so I did not have to leave by a certain time.

I walked into her new hospital room at Jersey Shore for the first time the following morning and felt both relief and stress. Jen was being monitored non-stop with an EEG with remote video monitoring, but there were even more machines hooked up to her now. Doctors were able to monitor her seizures in real time, so no one was able to stand in front of the video monitor. There were countless cables and sensors affixed to her head. Jen was still having some seizure activity, but it was not as frequent nor as severe. I got into the habit of asking the attending nurse if Jen had had any seizures the previous night. My heart sunk every time the answer was yes.

For the first couple of days at Jersey Shore, I had a schedule. First, I would drop the girls off at day care where everyone always asked about Jen. I would then make the twenty-minute drive up the Garden State Parkway to Jersey Shore so that I could sit with Jen for as long as I could. The hospital provided each CCU suite a reclining chair for visitors so that they could sleep next to the patient if they wanted. When I came into Jen's room, I would position the chair in a way that allowed me to lay out next to her and hold her left hand. There were a few times that I managed to doze off, holding her hand in mine. That small act evoked feelings of warmth and tenderness that I will remember forever.

I would spend a few hours sitting by Jen's side each day. I would then return home for a while before picking the girls up from school. By this point, I would be physically exhausted, even though I fell asleep some days in Jen's room. Thankfully, Jen's parents were there to help with the girls playing with them, giving them dinner, bathing them and watching them so that I could do what I had to do.

Every night after dinner, I would travel back to the hospital, letters and cards in hand, climb back in the recliner, hold Jen's hand, and slowly read each one as I tried to hold back the tears. I would make sure we had complete privacy, or as close to it as possible. I would also shut her suite door and pull the curtain around, so we could be by ourselves, even though we were not completely alone. I was not allowed to sit in front of the camera that was recording her seizures. I would have to pause numerous times during my readings because the emotions were so overwhelming to me that I had to stop just so I could breathe.

I would stay with Jen for as long as I felt I could. I wanted to have enough time with her and not feel rushed and still be able to see the girls before they fell asleep at night. I knew Jen would have wanted me to be there for our daughters; and it was important that the girls saw me, knowing that they still had their father.

By the time I got home each night, I was not only physically exhausted, but also mentally and spiritually drained. I had nothing left to give to anyone. I slept, but it was not a restful sleep. I woke up several times throughout the night, either due to nightmares, sheer panic, or because of the dread knowing that I would have to repeat the same events the next day.

This was around the same time that I met the three hospital social workers assigned to Jen's case. The first one specialized in children with grief. The second one was a social worker assigned to assist family members, in general, who had loved ones in the hospital with the ailments just like Jen's. The third was a nurse practitioner who assisted the other two social workers. There were a couple of times they sat with me and asked if there was anything, they could do specifically for me with the girls. It was the nurse practitioner who was advocating for me, trying to get the information I needed so that I could make the best decisions possible regarding Jen.

A few days after Jen arrived at Jersey Shore, I was told that the neurologist wanted to meet with Jen's parents and me regarding Jen's condition and his recommendations about her treatment. Her seizures were not fully controlled at that point, and Jen remained sedated and was not responding to any stimulus that the medical staff had given her. If she lived, I feared she was going to remain in a permanent vegetative state, and I would have to make certain decisions about whether or not to keep her on life support. This is a decision that **NO** spouse or partner should ever have to make.

The girls were in school when the Jersey Shore medical team met with Jen's parents and me. The neurologist said he had reviewed Jen's case from the time she arrived at Ocean Medical Center to that moment and reaffirmed my ultimate fears: Jen was brain dead and would never recover. She was never going to speak in her voice again, move any part of her body on her own, hold the girls in her arms, tell me that she loved me, or even breathe on her own. The Jen I knew and loved for so many years was gone forever. His recommendation was to let nature take its course.

The three of us began to weep uncontrollably. We knew that Jen would have to be taken off life support. We all knew that Jen would not have wanted to remain in a vegetative state for the rest of her life. The woman that we all knew was never coming back.

The social workers and doctors told us that they would give us some time alone in the conference room to absorb everything. I told Jen's parents that I wanted to take on the responsibility of planning and paying for all of Jen's arrangements. I already knew what Jen wanted because, ironically, we had discussed what we would do when one of us passed on and what we wanted as a couple for our final resting place. I told them what I had to do to accommodate Jen's wishes, and Jen's parents listened to me and agreed. They started making phone calls to their immediate family, and I did the same to my father and sister.

Jen's parents suggested that I ask the hospital's social worker to call our local church and a nearby funeral home. The priest from our church agreed to come out to Jen's bedside to administer her last rites that afternoon, and the funeral home agreed to have a representative meet with me at the funeral home right after I was done with the priest. All of this was going to be done before the girls were picked up from daycare.

The priest, a very pleasant and older gentleman, appeared at Jen's suite rather quickly, probably within an hour of the time he was contacted by the social worker. I prayed with the priest that Jen's soul would be forgiven for all of her sins (even though Jen was a saint to me), and that her suffering would soon be relieved from any pain. This seemed so very surreal. I had gone from having some hope that Jen would be brought home to hoping that she would pass peacefully, and that she would be ready to transition to some type of afterlife.

The priest took approximatively ten to fifteen minutes to anoint her, did his best to comfort me, and informed me to contact the church to make the preparations for Jen's funeral mass. It was a very strange situation to me. Why would God, so benevolent, loving, and caring, not want to stop and heal someone like Jen, who had nothing but love, compassion, and warmth in her heart? Why not save this woman so that she could watch her children grow?

I thanked the priest for his time and made my way to the funeral home. At this point, I wanted to make these decisions, so that I could allow myself to drown in my grief. One of the first questions the funeral home director asked me was if Jen and I had chosen our final resting place. Of course, we had not. Jen was only 35 years old, and this was not the kind of thing that 35-year-olds who were raising a family thought about. Though we had talked about this, we had never acted on it.

I knew three things I wanted for Jen: 1) I wanted her final resting place to be in Monmouth County, New Jersey, 2) I wanted her as close to the ocean as possible, and 3) I wanted her above ground in a mausoleum. The funeral director placed a call to the director of a nearby catholic cemetery, and he agreed to see me. Meanwhile I was able to complete some of the initial paperwork, pick out a casket for Jen, and managed to finalize some of the other arrangements, as best we could not knowing *when* she was going to pass away. We did agree, however, that when the time came for her to be transported from the hospital to the funeral home, we would communicate with each other so that the transition would be smooth.

I left the funeral home and made my way to the catholic cemetery. The cemetery director met me and took me through the different pricing of plots: in ground versus above ground. Strangely, it was pretty easy to make the necessary decisions because I knew what would be fitting for Jen. I also knew that I was not only making arrangements for Jen, but also for me. As long as I knew that Jen and I would be together forever, I would be happy.

The director showed me a tomb that was at eye level, facing east towards the direction of the ocean, and with a bench almost directly in front of the tomb. I knew this was it. He did not have to show me anything more. I paid the deposit on the tomb, and left the cemetery, and, like always, went home to be with the girls. I had to be a father to my daughters.

This was one of the roughest and darkest days in my life—hearing that Jen was not going to make a recovery, coming to grips that I would have to live a life without my wife, and ultimately make final arrangements for her death. But there was still one more task, and it was going to be one of the most difficult and painful things I would ever have to do: tell my daughters that they would never see their mother again.

It was actually two days before I mustered up the courage to tell the girls. True, I wanted to disrupt their lives as little as possible. But I'm not going to lie. I procrastinated in telling them because I was scared. When Jen collapsed, I had told the girls she had dropped a pot on her foot. Now I had to tell them she was never coming home, and I did not know the best way to break this horrible news to them.

Jen's parents, brother, sister-in-law, and uncle from North Carolina, who drove up to see Jen in the hospital that day, were all with me. We gathered in a circle around the girls, and I told the girls that I wanted to tell them something and they had to sit on my lap. I did not lie, nor did I speak in the medical jargon that had thrown at me for the past two weeks. I simply told them that mommy was very sick and that she was going to leave us and go heaven. There were a few moments where the girls shockingly did not say anything; they just sat on my lap absorbing everything. Then, both jumped off my lap, hysterically crying, and ran into their room. I ran after them, followed them into there and closed the door. I did my best to console them, but their world had just been shattered.

I finally convinced Giada to take a walk with me—a lot of houses on our block had put up their Christmas lights and that would calm her down. I grabbed a small bottle of rum, told Jen's family that we were going for a walk, got our coats on, went outside, and held Giada in my arms as we headed down the sidewalk.

Our next-door neighbor, John, was outside wrapping garland around his light posts, saw me, and asked what had happened. He knew Jen was in the hospital but did not know her prognosis. John immediately invited us into his home to see his mother and their golden doodle. They had a huge Christmas tree in their living room, and the house was beautifully decorated for the holidays. John told his mother, Juliette, what had happened. She immediately hugged and held Giada, consoling her as best she could.

Jen's brother came over to John and Juliette's house shortly thereafter with Rossella. Juliette gave the girls juice boxes and snacks, and they were playing with the dog, acting as if the news I had just told them did not phase them. It brought me some much-needed joy and relief to see the girls smiling and having a little bit of fun.

We stayed at my neighbors' house for longer than I thought we would; the girls were having so much fun playing with their dog and watching television with Juliette. The time I spent with my neighbors meant the world to me because it showed me that even in the worst of times, when you feel like the world is at odds with you, you get to see how great some people really are, and how big their hearts can open up to you. John and Juliette managed to give me something that only a handful of people were able to do during this time. They provided me with a respite from my grief and a distraction from my collapsing world. I watched my daughters act like normal kids (and I use this term very loosely because these were extremely abnormal circumstances for all of us), and it gave me a little bit of hope. No matter what was going to happen, my kids would be resilient. And, they would bounce back, no matter how long it would take them.

We made our way back home, and I gave the girls a

bath and told them again that no matter what happens, they would always have their daddy as well as their mommy watching over them. This was the first of the many times I would have to come to terms with the reality that Jen would no longer be physically present in their lives; she would live on only in their hearts, minds, and spirits. They, of course, asked me the obvious questions that a couple of four-year-old kids would ask: "Why is mommy not coming home? Where is she going? Why can't she come home?"

Each question felt like a punch in my gut. This was tearing me apart, but I did my best to hold it together. When Jen's family returned from eating dinner at a local diner, I settled the girls down for the night and made my way back to the hospital. I knew that I could not waste anytime saying my final goodbyes to Jen.

That night at the hospital, I just sat there and balled my eyes out. I knew now that my time with Jen was limited, and that I had to cherish every moment I had left with my wife. The reality that Jen was dying had begun to sink in. Still, I felt disbelief that my life was taking this turn.

I brought my usual number of cards and love letters to Jen, though I now knew she was unable to respond. Even then, I held unto a sliver of hope at the possibility of a miraculous recovery that would prove all the doctors wrong.

I stayed at the hospital for as long as I could, kissed Jen on her cheeks, just like always, and made my way back down the Garden State Parkway. When I got home, I walked into my bedroom and crawled into my bed.

This was one of many days that I welcomed closing my eyes to the world.

Jen was an organ donor, so the process of harvesting her organs had to be started immediately. I was informed by the New Jersey Sharing Network, a non-profit organization that promotes organ donation, that once her breathing tube was removed, she would only have sixty minutes to pass on if her organs were going to be donated. Even though I did not agree with Jen's decision about organ donation, I had no choice but to comply. Plus, it was on her driver's license. The only request I made to the doctors and to the Sharing Network was that they were to leave Jen with her eyes. I was not at all comfortable with the possibility of Jen being put to rest without her eyes.

Jen's life support was to be removed, and all the paperwork with the Sharing Network completed. The plan was to remove her breathing tube the following evening. I spent the next two afternoons with Jen, trying to find the most appropriate way to say goodbye to her. Say goodbye to her? How the hell was I even supposed to do that? How could anyone possibly say good bye to the person with whom you were supposed to spend the rest of your life? This was completely unfathomable to me. Despite the lack of clear thoughts, little sleep, and the overwhelming fear and grief, I burned an image of Jen into my mind. It was the afternoon before the day her life support would be removed. I held her hand. Her fingers were interlaced with mine. I took a picture with my cell phone of just our two hands. That picture will forever be on my phone. I think I kissed Jen about a dozen times that afternoon, and I told her that I would see her again. I also told her that she had to come back and told her that she had to come back to me, live inside of me, and guide me. When I walked out of the hospital room, I never felt more disgusted in my entire life. The hope that had driven me for the past two weeks was drained out of me—gone completely.

I decided that I did not want to be present when Jen's breathing tube was removed. I had witnessed too many horrific events in the past weeks, and I did not want to spend my last moments with Jen watching her struggle to breath. Jen's family, however, did decide to be there, and I stayed with the girls. Somehow, I managed to stick with our routine and get them to bed on time, but all the while I had my cell phone right by my side, anxiously awaiting updates. One hour after life support was removed, Jen was still breathing on her own. It was then we were told that Jen would not be able to donate her organs after all—yet another sucker punch to my gut. Something that Jen had wanted to do, a way for her to help other people, had now become impossible.

Sometime around 11 p.m. Jen's family returned to my house, but without Jen's mom, who had made the decision to remain at Jen's side. We were told that if anything happened to Jen, she would call us, regardless of the time.

Early the next morning, I received a call from the hospital asking my permission to move Jen up to the hospice on the sixth floor where she would remain until she passed. She would *die in comfort*—such an ironic play on words. I granted my permission, and Jen was moved to hospice later that day. She was given a private suite that overlooked most of Neptune, New Jersey. From the distance you could see where the buildings and homes ended, and the ocean met the sand.

I decided I would visit Jen one more time while she was in hospice, even though I had already said my goodbyes. I would have regretted not doing so, and I didn't want to live with regret about anything involving Jen.

When I arrived at her bedside, Jen's mother was there with her. She had spent the night in Jen's suite, sleeping on a chair. At this point, Jen was off all life support and just receiving a morphine drip. There were no more tubes coming out of her mouth, no EEG wires attached to her head, and no other machines beeping non-stop in the background. It was just Jen—lying there, eyes closed. This image of Jen just lying there without the life support was rather beautiful to me. It was Jen, not a machine. Still, I knew within a few minutes of being there that the spirit—the warmth -- that had made Jen the woman I loved for so many years was not in that room. It had left me the night she collapsed at home, but at least I had the comfort of seeing Jen one more time in her natural state.

The next day, December 11th was a Monday, and just like 9/11 or the day Jen collapsed at home, it will be a day I will never forget. I will forever be able to recall everything that happened to me. That morning, as I was preparing to take Giada and Rossella to our spot on the beach in Avon-by-the-Sea, I learned that Jen's fever had spiked to 107 degrees and her breathing was extremely labored. The end was coming. I knew I had to go to the cemetery and make my final payment for the mausoleum immediately so Jen could be moved into it. I needed to know that I had done everything I could to make Jen's funeral a tribute to the wonderful woman she was and the move to her final resting place graceful and filled with peace.

I made my way to the cemetery; took one last look at the tomb I had picked and knew I had made the right choice. I knew it was a perfect resting spot because there was a bench directly in front of her tomb, the only bench in the cemetery that would allow me to sit down when I would visit her.

The girls and I then made our way to Avon, so that we could be at one of our happiest places during what was going to be one of the darkest moments of our lives. We had just entered Belmar, the neighboring town to Avon, when I received a call from Jen's mother. "I need you to come pick me up," she said. That was our code to say that Jen had passed away. Nineteen days—just 19 days to turn our family's lifetime upside down, devastated beyond the point of recognition.

I screamed and immediately broke down. Giada and Rossella began to cry. My world was shattered. My heart had been broken in a million pieces. The woman whom I loved, honored, and cherished for seventeen years was no longer physically on earth. I managed to compose myself enough to tell Jen's mother that I would pick her up at the valet entrance of Jersey Shore in about 20 minutes. At that moment, there was only one place where the girls and I had to be.

It only took about five minutes to get to the Garfield Avenue beach entrance in Avon. I left my cell phone in the car and walked with the girls out onto the sand. It was a bright, sunny, and cold day. There was hardly anyone on the boardwalk or on the beach. The privacy of the setting brought me some peace as we made our way out approximately halfway between the boardwalk and the breaking waves. I then kneeled so I could talk eye level with both of my daughters. "Mommy is now in heaven," I said, "and this spot on the beach will be the place where mommy's spirit will always be with you—where she will always be watching over you. We will come to this spot as long as we can." I hugged each of them as I cried, and then we made our way back to the car. The girls sobbed; they knew that their mommy was in heaven and that she was never coming home.

After buckling the girls back in their car seats, I started making the necessary but difficult phone calls: my father, sister, Jen's friends, Jen's boss, my friend Dennis, who said that he would tell my boss and others at my job, the owner of the girls' day care, and my other friends. I made all these calls from the beach. Each phone call was extremely quick, lasting one to two minutes. Those I did not call, I texted that Jen was no longer with us.

I then drove to the hospital and picked Jen's mother up at the valet stand. She had gathered her belongings in plastic bags, as well as the couple of items that belonged to Jen. She hugged the girls and we made our way home.

My phone immediately blew up with phone calls and text messages of sympathy. When we arrived home, I called the funeral home director, but someone from the hospital had already called him to say that Jen had passed. We were told that her body would be held in the hospital for a while because her last attending doctor had requested an autopsy. I was pleased to hear this, because the passing of a healthy, 35-year old woman from cardiac arrest was not the norm.

As the day wore on, it was still difficult to grasp all that had happened and to fully comprehend that Jen was gone. We replayed the events of the last 19 days and cried a lot. My mind began to race thinking about all that Jen would be missing: watching the girls hit their milestones, vacations, family get-togethers, holidays. All of this would never be the same again, nor would have as much meaning now that Jen was gone.

Additionally, I began to realize how insignificant my previous worries were in life. Not getting a supervisor to agree with me on a business decision, getting cut off by another driver, having to shell out money for unforeseen car repairs, or even having a fight with a family member or friend all now seemed petty to me. Everything paled in comparison to what we had endured and beared witness to throughout this whole ordeal.

There are still plenty of times that I reexamine the events of this time period and have no idea how I survived. I now understand that it does not matter how I survived, but that I did, and that Giada and Rossella survived as well. Somehow, I managed to endure a tremendous amount of anguish and misery that was traumatic in so many ways. As a result of enduring the pain and trauma of watching Jen suddenly fall ill and slowly die, I do feel as though I am a stronger person, a smarter man, and a more loving father. I have been told that it was remarkable how I was able to focus on the positives from this experience. But to me, it is not remarkable to have these different viewpoints. They simply occurred naturally within me.

Most people do not experience these life altering events in their lives, but in 19 short days my life had radically changed. So had my outlook. I had lost my soulmate, the woman with whom I wanted to spend the rest of my life. The horror of this had given me a new perspective about being alive on this planet, made me see what is truly important in life, and forced me to acknowledge how I should spend the rest of my life. There would be other events that shaped my new outlook, but clearly it would be everything I saw, said, and underwent in those 19 days that redefined who I now am as a person—and, perhaps surprisingly—for the better, not for the worse.

5

Fallout

December 12th—the day after—was a day I never thought I would have to experience in my life. What was I supposed to do now? Waking up as a widower honestly did not phase me. The shock of the finality was still as strong as it had been on that fateful night when Jen took her last breaths in our home. I had slept with Jen's robe that night, using it as a blanket. It still had some of her scent on it. I wanted to preserve her clothing and other personal items so that her fragrance would never leave me.

But right then—actually, from the moment I learned Jen would be taken off life support to let nature take its course—I was hell bent on making sure that Jen would have a fitting final tribute. I was on a mission to ensure that every detail of her viewing and funeral service was perfect. I wanted her to be remembered in a way that most embodied the way she lived, and planning and coordinating her funeral were going to be the very last thing I was going to be able to physically do for her. The thought of never buying a birthday gift or anniversary present for her was so painful to me. I repeatedly kept Jen's parents and other family members, informed, but I did not want any help from anyone. I had to know that I was taking care of my soulmate when she was no longer able to care for herself. Jen would have done the same for me.

I wanted Jen's parents to know that I was doing the best for their daughter. Our meeting with the funeral home director was surreal to me. We were still waiting to find out when the hospital was going to release Jen's body to the funeral home.

After we left the funeral home, someone from the hospital called to inform me that the county medical examiner declined to conduct an autopsy, because Jen's death did not warrant that level of scrutiny. This put me into a tailspin. Why would there not be an autopsy when we were told by her last attending doctor that he would not release her body until one was completed? First no organ donation. Now this. I immediately got into my car and drove back up to the hospital. My emotions were so heightened that I began to visibly shake when I parked the car.

I arrived at the front desk and requested to speak to the supervising nurse of the pathology department. I was mentally preparing to go into battle. I was ready to refuse to leave the hospital until I had the whole ordeal straightened out to my satisfaction—even if it meant I got arrested. As ridiculous as I later realized I was behaving, I actually told Jen's mother to get a good lawyer for me so I would be out of jail in time for Jen's funeral.

The supervisor came down to the hospital lobby and

met with me. She reassured me that despite the ruling from the county medical examiner, the hospital would be conducting the autopsy later that week. I thanked her and immediately left the hospital. When I got back to the car, I proceeded to have my first of many panic attacks. My emotions were swallowing me up whole, overtaking my body like a tidal wave. The crying was intense, my breathing was heavy, and then I began to get sick in the parking lot. Knowing that Jen's body was somewhere inside the building in front of me, knowing that it was going to be dissected within days was overwhelming and almost impossible to comprehend. Everyone kept telling me that Jen's body was a vessel and that it was not really her—not the soul of her and all the wonderful things she had accomplished and represented. That notion provided no comfort to me then and affords no solace to me now. When you spend time with the person you love, you want to hold, touch, caress, and even remember every inch of your loved one's body. You are drawn to that person. You create a physical bond with her. You hold hands, feel her warmth when she lies next to you, and you even get caught up with the tiniest details about that person. For me, I remembered how I would run my fingers through her hair, getting my fingers stuck in her curls. All of these wonderful and priceless things that I wanted to do for the rest of my life with her, were no longer possible. To compound the pain, the thought that she would be subjected to all of these pathology tests was gut wrenching, especially that her brain was going to be closely examined and tested in numerous ways. These tests were going to uncover how bad her anoxic brain injury was as a result of the cardiac arrest.

It was a couple of days before the funeral home received notification that the autopsy was going to be completed. I had arranged for Jen to be viewed for one day, Sunday, December 17th, and then for her funeral mass and entombment to take place the following day, December 18th. All this would be just one week before Christmas.

I was informed of the day and time Jen would be picked up by the funeral home. I had specifically requested that the hearse drive on Ocean Avenue in Avon-by-the-Sea and stop right on Garfield Avenue. I received a text message from the funeral director, telling me the exact moment she was there. When I got the text message, I was driving my car and pulled over to the shoulder because I burst out in tears. I knew that this would be Jen's very last time at her favorite place on earth.

In the days leading up to the wake, there were several tasks that I had to take care of, both related and not related to the funeral. I had picked out a floral spray for her casket—a beach theme with all flowers I knew she liked. I had three starfish added to the arrangement, one for me and one for each of the girls. I made sure there were no carnations because Jen, as well as my mother, hated carnations. Her mass cards had the image of footprints walking in the sand, adjacent to ocean waves for her love of the beach. It seemed very appropriate to me.

I knew that there were several things that had to be with Jen in her casket. Pictures of the girls and me were obvious, specifically a picture of the four of us from our trip to Saint Lucia from October 2017. There were also the remains of the cat who was her pet when she was a teenager, along with the remains of our cat, Anastasia, who passed away from cancer while we were on vacation in Saint Lucia. Jen had wanted Anastasia's cremated remains to be kept with me when I passed away, but right now that did not seem right to me. She loved Anastasia as much as I did, so I made the decision to give Anastasia to Jen.

The most important thing the girls and I gave to Jen to take to heaven with her was **Jen's** piece of Avon, her little piece of heaven on earth. I had gone to Walmart and purchased a small glass mason jar with an aqua blue rubber liner which the girls and I filled with sand from our spot. I knew Jen had to take a little bit of Avon with her on her journey, and again, this was one of the last physical things I could do for her.

While I gathered the sand, the girls strolled down the beach, staying close to the frigid ocean, collecting shells and rocks they gathered to give to their mother for her trip to heaven. When the time came to place the shells in the casket, I laid them in Jen's coffin next to her. I had promised the girls that mommy would indeed know that the shells were from them.

I knew that I had to profess not only my love for Jen in her eulogy, but I also had the responsibility of providing some closure to all of our family and friends. I had literally lost count of how many times, people said to me, "I don't know what to say." To me, it was fine that they said this. But just as with the constant, "how are you doing?" question, I did not know how to respond. I was determined that Jen's funeral would allow me to help people begin to heal from this devastating loss.

I worked on Jen's eulogy for days, making numerous revisions as I read and reread it. I did get to the point at which I felt it was able to convey what I wanted to say to everyone. It was not perfect, but I knew then as I do now, that nothing I said would fully capture all of my thoughts, expectations, and experiences.

The day before the wake, the funeral director informed me that Jen was laid out in the viewing room at the funeral home. I requested time alone with her, before anyone else saw her the next day. Those fifteen minutes I had with her were very peaceful and meaningful and allowed me the comfort and solace that I desperately needed. I cried uncontrollably. I spoke to her, and just stared with wonderment at how beautiful she was. This would be the very last time that I would be completely alone with Jen, and I had to be fully present every second.

This precious time alone with Jen was my secret…my gift to myself—my private "see you later," not good-bye.

The morning of Jen's wake I began to mentally prepare myself for the emotional tidal wave that was going to crash upon me. I knew that I had to take things literally one moment at a time and keep reminding myself that I was going to survive this in one piece.

When Jen's parents, Emad, Sara, and I got to the funeral home that morning, we had our private viewing with Jen. By this time, the room was filled with flowers from family, friends, and our employers. There was also a television screen that was rotating through twenty or so pictures of Jen with various family members and friends. I had picked the pictures and reviewed them with Jen's parents prior to the wake. We were given as much time as we wanted to with Jen. We all knew that there were people gathering in the lobby of the funeral home, but we did not care; this was our time. The girls stayed with Josh and Nicole, who were very gracious, and decided to take the girls to a local children's museum while we were at the wake.

One of the first people that showed up, even before visiting hour begun, was my friend Dennis. He had driven five hours that morning to make sure that he was there for me and my family. He had told me that he had hardly gone to funerals since his father died years before. I was honored that he came all the way from Berkshire County, Massachusetts, to pay his respects and to show how much of a friend he really was to me. One lesson that I learned very quickly, and Dennis is a prime example, is that you absolutely know from an event like this the who people are truly your friends as opposed to which people say they are your friends but quickly forget about you when the dust settles. It is surprising how those individuals who you never expected to be true friends become great friends to you as a result of a tragedy. Dennis was someone who repeatedly had my six—had my back when times were rough—and unequivocally had my best interests at heart. A friend like Dennis is something that people always want in life, but they do not always get. Even though he is twenty years older than I am (sorry Dennis), and he is sometimes mistaken for my father when we go out to dinner (sorry again Dennis), I would do anything for him, and I always refer to him as my brother.

The afternoon session of Jen's wake was literally packed with people. I had to sit in the lobby of the funeral home because there were too many people in the viewing room. I felt overwhelmed very quickly that afternoon. Jen's family from North Carolina, Illinois, and Pennsylvania, came to the wake; all of my family from New York and Northern New Jersey came, as well as former co-workers whom I had not seen for years. Parents from the girls' day care, as well as the day care owner and teachers also came to the wake. For those two hours, probably more than one hundred people showed up.

I did find myself sneaking out to my car on occasion for a shot of whiskey or rum (I did come prepared). I did not drink enough to get drunk, but the fact remained that I was a grieving widower. It was important to me to have people distinguish needing a drink to lessen my anxiety versus having individuals thinking I was drinking for pleasure.

My immediate family, as well as Jen's immediate family, went out to dinner in between the afternoon and evening viewing sessions. I gave a round of Jen's favorite drink, a White Russian, to all who wanted it with their dinners. I know that this is what Jen would have wanted—a celebration of her life, with everyone enjoying being together instead of continuously crying.

The evening viewing was just as busy and probably another fifty to seventy-five people came to pay their respects. I was extremely grateful for the outpouring of love. I saw it as a testament to the impact Jen had had on so many people's lives and the way she had touched so many others with her generosity and kindness. It was a testament to how much she was loved by so many people.

I was one of the last people to leave Jen that night, compelled as I was to stay with her as long as I could. During that quiet alone time, I reflected on the day and was taken by a memory of our time together.

Jen and I loved watching the movie *Goodfellas*. It's a classic New York mafia movie with Robert DeNiro, Joe Pesci, and Ray Liotta. What is there not to like? Jen was a big Ray Liotta fan, and she especially loved two things about Goodfellas: how young Ray Liotta looked in the movie and wedding scene with Ray Liotta and Lorraine Bracco's characters, the Hills. Jen loved that scene, and there was one line that sticks out with me now. Karen Hill said, "At the end of the night I felt like I was drunk," and this line resonated with me because that is exactly how I felt at the end of that night. In a short period of time (just a few hours as a matter of fact), I had so many thoughts and emotions swirling around inside of me. By the end of that Sunday night, I shook hands with close to two hundred people, spoke to people I had only seen maybe once in my life (or in some cases, not at all), and I was not even sure what I had said to them. I could not even comprehend how I was able to breathe or walk throughout the entire day. It was as if I had had about ten or twelve drinks in a three-hour period, and I was barely able to coherently function. Looking back on that day now, however, I am struck—even impressed—that I did it. Getting through Jen's wake was indeed a milestone—one of the many that I've accomplished since November 2017.

The next morning, Jen's funeral, I woke up knowing that this was going to be a very long, mentally draining day for me. I had arranged for a limousine to pick Jen's parents, brother, sister-in-law, my daughters, and me up at my house and chauffeur us to the different stops we would make throughout the day.

When we arrived at the funeral home, we were part of a group of about 30 people, who had congregated for the short prayer service that was going to be given by the funeral home director. The prayer service only lasted about ten minutes. When the time came for Jen to be moved to the hearse, I watched as the funeral home director lowered Jen into the casket and closed the coffin. Jen's father and I stood motionless and quiet while Jen's body was placed lower into the casket. I did my best to etch those couple of minutes in my head, because that would be the last time I would physically see Jen's face, and this was absolutely heartbreaking and devastating to me.

The funeral home staff then placed her casket on a cart and wheeled her to the all-white Rolls Royce hearse. I held the girls' hands and walked behind Jen to the hearse. I had to be as physically close to her as possible during this entire time.

The procession of cars led by the hearse, then our limousine, made its way from the funeral home to our parish church, about a fifteen-minute ride through the side streets of Wall Township and then eventually Howell.

A crowd was already assembled outside the church. As I walked hand-in-hand with my daughters as Jen was moved inside, I saw that perhaps over one hundred people were seated in the pews.

Just like at the funeral home, I was right behind her, every step of the way. I held my head high, doing my best not to break out in tears, but I knew if I did, it would have been fine.

My typed eulogy rested securely in my jacket pocket as Giada, Rossella and I walked to the first pew and all the way at the end. Throughout the traditional Catholic mass, I was inundated with a surreal feeling. Was this really happening? I stared at Jen's coffin positioned in the center aisle. I was in shock. Jen was gone, and a life without her was going to be my new reality.

When the priest delivered his homily, he reiterated how difficult it would be for any of us to understand Jen's untimely death. It just occurred the way and time that it did. I will never remember exactly what he said, but I will remember that this tried his best to comfort every person in that church.

At the conclusion of the mass, the priest signaled to me that it was time for the eulogies. Emad had also prepared a eulogy and I told him to go first. He approached the pulpit and did a tremendous job. He made reference to one of Jen's favorite movies, Pollyanna, and suggested that everyone in attendance should play the Glad Game, having each person point out one thing that they were happy for on that day.

Then it was my turn to speak. Normally I would have been nervous, but at Jen's funeral mass this did not happen. I was deeply aware of my responsibility to deliver the perfect eulogy for Jen and provide at least some rudimentary sense of closure and healing to everyone who had come to the church to pay tribute to Jen. I explained what type of person Jen was, what life meant to her, and most importantly, what her love meant to me. I shared a portion of a love letter I had written to her fourteen years earlier. It best explained my feelings for her throughout the time that we were together:

My love for you is like a snowfall. When I step outside, snowflakes fall on me and remind me of all of the memories I'd shared with you. Each snowflake is unique, like every memory that I've had with you. And when I step outside, the snow keeps building up, just like my love for you as each day passes.

The service concluded following my eulogy, and I made sure that the girls and I were the first ones to leave the church and watch Jen's casket being returned to the hearse. I was approached by people who I did not even know were in the church. Two of my former co-workers had driven down from Connecticut, three and a half hours away, just to sit in the fifty-minute church service. There were also a considerable number of Jen's co-workers there, and some of them approached me and said that they were moved by what I said at the pulpit. I simply told them that those words had to be spoken, and those were the only things that could be said that were truly appropriate and meaningful to me.

The procession of about twenty or so cars, including the hearse and limousine, made its way through the side streets of Howell, back into Wall Township, and on to the cemetery. The procession had to make its way through two major intersections in Wall and the funeral director had made arrangements with the Wall Township Police to block traffic so that the procession would not be broken up as it wove its way through that part of town.

When all of the cars arrived at the cemetery, everyone parked around the mausoleum. The funeral director and the deacon from the church walked beside the casket. I accompanied my daughters to the first pew. Unlike at the church service when I sat on the on the far end of the pew away from the coffin, I sat in the mausoleum directly next to Jen. I knew that this would be the very last time that I would be this close to her body without a slab of marble between us.

The deacon spoke, and then everyone made their way up to the coffin to say one last goodbye to Jen. I sat with the girls and watched as each person walked behind the casket, some crying, some holding it together as best they could. When the service concluded, Jen's brother and parents stood up, touched the coffin, and made their way out of the mausoleum. As selfish as it may have seemed, I again wanted to be the last one to say goodbye to Jen. I stood up and threw my arms around the casket, kissed it, and told her that I loved her.

I slowly made my way back to the limousine. I was completely drained. I took a deep breath to calm down as I watched Jen's coffin being wheeled to the mausoleum. No more breathing tubes. No more life support. And no more gut-wrenching coughs. No more waiting to hear about test results and a prognosis. Jen was resting in peace now, facing east, as close to Avon-by-the-Sea as possible.

6

Skipping Christmas

This was my new reality, my new world. I was walking into it without the woman I looked to for support, guidance, and love. I had just laid my wife and the mother of my children to rest. I was not going to wake up and realize this had been a bad dream.

Frightening as this was, being a widower and a single parent was now my life. I was petrified, but I knew that I had to pull it together as best I could for Rossella and Giada. I now had to give them love for both Jen and me, and that didn't even begin to take into account the many additional challenges and obstacles that I would soon have to face—challenges that would redefine and mold the person I would eventually become, both as a father and a man.

It was ironic that the holidays were always the happiest time of year for me, and, now, they transformed into something horrific. Christmas 2017 had no joy, no meaning, and no happiness. Jen was laid to rest on

December 19th, and in the days that followed, it was extremely hard to focus on anything associated with celebrating the holidays. Every night, I watched as neighbors turned on their Christmas lights. *What is wrong with them?* I found myself asking. *How could they celebrate Christmas?* Then, reality set in. Those families had not just lost their soulmate. Of course, they were celebrating. They had not suffered the tremendous loss that I had endured, and they deserved the right to enjoy the holidays.

And then there were my daughters. They still were entitled to have the best Christmas possible, even though I did not want to do anything festive. In the days leading up to December 25th, I simply allowed myself to shut down. I focused on nothing beyond taking care of Rossella and Giada. It was simply too much to comprehend having anything that resembled a normal life.

Every November we loved getting into the holiday spirit by watching Christmas movies. *Christmas with the Kranks*, an adaptation of the book, *Skipping Christmas,* was a feel-good movie, and one of our favorites. Jen and I always asked ourselves how anyone could want to "skip Christmas?" This routinely baffled us because everything about the holidays *was* wonderful, emphasis on the word *was*. I had finally gotten an answer. For the first time in my life, I wanted to "skip Christmas."

Everyone told me that I would have to experience a "year of firsts," basically one year of going through all of the holidays, anniversaries, birthdays, and other special occasions without Jen before I could feel better. The widows and widowers that I would eventually meet in my support group said this as well. Christmas 2017 was my *first of the firsts*.

Rossella, Giada, Jen's parents, and I stayed the night of December 23rd at Jen's uncle's house in Morris County, New Jersey. The girls got to play with their two cousins. Then on the afternoon of December 24th, we all made our way back to my house in Monmouth County. My good friends, Adam and Terri, and their son Dylan, who was in the girls' day care class, stopped by with Christmas presents for the girls and a nice bottle of Chavis for me. It meant a great deal to me that they took time out of their Christmas Eve to come to my house and spend a little time with us.

Once the girls went to bed, Jen's parents put all of Rossella and Giada's presents under the Christmas tree in the living room. They made sure that the girls were going to have a great Christmas, even though none of the adults wanted to celebrate. I was thankful that they were there to guarantee that the girls had gotten everything they asked for Christmas.

Christmas Day came and went, and I am proud to say that I survived. One important lesson learned: It is okay if survival is as good as it can get. It was part of my journey. There was no right or wrong way to feel. I was now a widower. It was vital to be in survival mode to overcome many obstacles and challenges, and Christmas 2017, was just the first of many that I would be forced to overcome to survive in my new reality.

7

Bottom Falling Out

We "celebrated" Christmas. Then there was my birthday on December 26th. When it came to my birthday, I had already told everyone, "No presents. No cake." Then there was New Years which was rapidly approaching.

Typically, I hated New Years because it not only ended the holiday fun but also meant I had to take down all the outdoor lights and decorations. In 2017, however, I was ecstatic when the year finally ended. Still, this January, I struggled to develop a routine or find a purpose, but there were some days that I found it difficult to complete even the simplest of tasks. Getting the girls to school, taking care of chores around the house, and even getting the girls ready for bed at night seemed like Herculean undertakings. There was not a day that went by that I didn't feel anxious, sad and depressed. These emotions were consuming me, eating me up inside, making me wonder if I was going to make it until the end of the day. I was suffering not only because of losing Jen, but also coming to grips with the fact that I had seen Jen die when she collapsed in front of me at home.

January 11th is a date I will always remember. It was a particularly cold morning. There seemed to be plenty of days when the temperature was below normal that winter, but I remember this day to be unusually cold. Looking back, it seemed that the temperature foreboded something about the day. I had several things to do which were going to be challenging, and then some additional things happened that turned out to be disturbing.   I had to pick the girls up early from day care, so that I could register them for kindergarten in the coming school year. I also was attending Jen's work holiday party that evening. Because of her love for the company, and for all her hard work and dedication, Jen was posthumously receiving an achievement award that I would accept on her behalf and address her colleagues.

It was a little difficult trying to explain to my daughters what kindergarten was going to be like for them, but I did my best telling them that it was a new school, and that they would meet new friends. I knew it would be difficult to explain that when they started kindergarten they would not be in the same school as their friends. Since my daughters were a year old, they were in the same day care center, with the same friends. All their friends lived in the next town, however, and would be attending a different school. This would have been a major adjustment for my kids under any circumstances. After all that had happened, even more so.

When I arrived home, I noticed that I received an email from the Human Resources Director, saying she and her supervisor wanted to speak to me about my position. I had Jen's mother take the girls downstairs to our family room, so I could make the phone call.

When I called the Human Resources Director, I was immediately placed on speaker with her and her supervisor, and that is when they broke the news: I was getting laid off because my position was eliminated. It was as if I was hit with a two-by-four and sucker punched in the gut. What they were saying did not sink in at first, but then I realized that I was going to lose another part of my life that made me who I was.

When I got off the phone, the shock wore off, and anger took over. I kept questioning how someone could say that to me, especially when that person knew that my job provided the layer of security that my daughters and I depended on during Jen's illness and following her death. This news was only one month to the day that Jen officially took her last breath. I absolutely felt that life was kicking me when I was on the ground writhing in pain and agony.

I was told that I was going to be paid for the rest of January and that I would be losing our health insurance as of February 1st, and that I would be eligible for unemployment at that time. I was told that this situation and ultimate decision of terminating my employment was not a reflection of my work at all, but rather that the needs of the company had shifted. I heard the words over the phone, but I did not believe anything that I was told. It was extremely hard not to take this personally, especially for someone in my situation. This was first time that I had been terminated by an employer, and not made the decision myself. No matter what the reason, it was a terrible feeling.

I was asked to send back all the company equipment that I had at my home and sign a termination agreement. I immediately took the letter and the equipment to my attorney, the same lawyer who was assisted me with the subpoena. She offered to facilitate further communications with my now former employer, making sure that everything that was about to happen to me was fair and not one sided. I was to have no further contact with the employer. She emphasized that I needed to let her handle it, so I did.

Telling my friends and family that I lost my job four weeks after losing Jen was not only difficult, but it was also embarrassing. I had to tell people that I sustained yet another loss in my life. Was my life going to turn into one huge disappointment? Was I going to continue to have setbacks? Would I ever climb out of this hole? Would there ever be an end in sight? I had very little time to ponder these questions on the afternoon of January 11th, 2018, because I still had to go to Jen's employer's holiday party that evening.

It had gotten dark before I had to leave for the holiday party. Jen had gone to this party every year since joining her employer seven years earlier. It was always at the same country club, and the same people always attended. Jen had the same comments every year: "The appetizers were good, the main course stunk, but it was great hanging out with everyone."

Of course, this year was completely different. I was going to the party, and I only knew a few people. I'd met some of her colleagues at Jen's funeral, but I had been in such a state of shock then that I did not remember their names now. At best, I would be guessing their names, or worse yet, require others to tell me who these people were.

I was ready though to accept the award and speak about Jen. I had already decided to avoid delivering a prepared speech. Instead, I was going to wing it and speak directly from my heart.

On the way up the Garden State Parkway that night, I blared my 80's music and thought about all of the events that had transpired earlier that day. *This is your life now. Disappointments and disasters are going to be your new norm.* I began to feel extremely hopeless. I was cursing the world and hating everyone I knew that was able to be at home with their spouses and kids, enjoying their lives. Then as I crossed over the Driscoll Bridge (some would argue that is the de facto boundary between North and South Jersey), I began to sense the warmth of Jen's spirit. It was present with me in the car, and this was the very first time that I felt that Jen was trying her best to comfort me in her own way, letting me know that she was there in the passenger seat next to me. Just like earlier that day when I was told that I was being laid off, this had the same intense feel but with an opposite effect. I was building up the strength so that I could be present for Jen at the party, talk about her to everyone, about how the girls and I were coping, how much Jen meant to me, but most importantly, thanking everyone for their kindness and compassion during my darkest hours.

I arrived at the party and had the car valeted by the country club's staff. I made my way inside and found Jen's boss, Kim, as well as the site director with whom

Jen had worked every day, Dara, and two of Jen's best friends, Pam and Samantha. They did their best to make me feel comfortable and introduced me to various people at the party.

The time had come for the awards presentation to begin. The head executive asked me again if I wanted to speak and I answered, "Absolutely." He explained to the approximately 300 people in the audience what the annual achievement award represented and why this year's award was being awarded to Jen. I was then introduced to everyone and given the plaque that had been engraved with Jen's name.

As I took the award in my hands, I gazed out at everyone in the banquet room. Everyone was standing for me, shoulder to shoulder in some cases, and I could not see the back of the room because of the sheer number of people in attendance. I had trouble deciding how close the microphone needed to be to my mouth; I did not want to be overbearing but I wanted to make sure everyone was able to hear me. After holding the microphone for about two seconds, I felt eerily comfortable, and the words were just flowing from my mind to my mouth. Just as with her eulogy, I felt a surprising joy that I was able to talk about Jen with such ease, telling everyone how much they helped me and our family. Most importantly, I conveyed my thoughts about how much they all meant to Jen and how much of an important role they played in the last few years of her life.

Jen loved her employer. She valued every day that she was able to contribute to the continued success and overall mission of the organization. As one of their quality management specialists, Jen was always assisting the site director and her staff on ways that improved the organization's delivery of clinical services and its efficiency of business practices. Jen's employer was a huge help to me when Jen suddenly fell ill. In fact, Jen's boss was the person responsible for creating the online fundraising page that provided me the financial support that I needed during her illness and would continue to help support my family.

My whole speech lasted maybe two minutes, but in those two minutes I spoke from my heart so that everyone could understand what I was feeling. Just like me, there were many people present at the party who were still in a state of shock and devastated by Jen's passing.

When the speech was over, I took my seat and decompressed. I felt as if I had just run a marathon. As I listened to the head executive give out the other awards, I had multiple people approach me thanking me for what I said about Jen, expressing their sympathies, and even sharing memories about working with Jen.

Before I left the party, Jen's site director had me sit in on a group picture of all the workers at their site. I was honored to be asked to be in the picture and represent Jen. I said my goodbyes after that and made my way home. My incredibly long and emotionally draining day had finally come to an end.

During my time speaking to everyone in that ballroom that night, I could not help thinking to myself that perhaps there were some people thinking "how is this man able to speak to us after what he has been through?" The old saying "what does not kill you makes you stronger," is also true for widows and widowers. Once a person endures the loss of partner, and in my case, the sudden and unexpected death of a spouse, you manage to find new strength and resolve to do almost anything.

Before Jen's death, I thought that public speaking was something that was daring and downright hard, something that I only wanted to do if I absolutely had to, but now it was something that was therapeutic and rewarding for me. In the months that followed, I would continue to figure out what my new strengths were, and how I would be presented with new opportunities that would make me a better man and father.

It is important for all widows and widowers to understand that there will be times when you will find yourself in situations that you never thought you could handle. Not only will you get through these trying times, but they may actually, in some cases, turn out to be beneficial to you, providing you with the strength you need to move forward on your journey, wherever it may take you.

8

First of the Firsts

In the days following the awards presentation, I began to experience what I felt were some of the real after effects of being a young widower. Jen was no longer a part of my life. She was not going to be coming through the front door at home, telling me about her day. I would no longer have her lying on the couch next to me at night, exhausted from her day at work and taking care of all of us. Jen was gone and never coming back. That was a fact, plain and simple.

The flashbacks of the night Jen collapsed were replaying on a loop in my mind, like a VHS tape. When this happened, I would instantly be transported back to that moment, sitting on the cold kitchen tile, having the cordless phone on the counter with the emergency operator telling me what to do, and most of all, hearing her gurgling, trying to breath, and shaking uncontrollably. I replayed the horror over and over. It was paralyzing. What was worse, I could not make the tape stop.

Getting a good night's sleep was out of the question.

I found it increasingly hard to both fall asleep on my own and then stay asleep throughout the night. My mind would race with thoughts of bleakness and despair. I also experienced a lot of survivor's guilt. *Why did the universe allow Jen to leave this world so suddenly, leaving behind the three people she cared most about? How does this make any sense if there is a God? How could this be part of any plan?*

The lack of restful and meaningful sleep started to catch up to me, physically and mentally. I turned to my doctor. He prescribed Ambien. Believe it or not, I asked the doctor, how it would feel when it took effect. The first night I took Ambien, I passed out within thirty minutes and slept through the night free of nightmares, mental anguish, and most importantly, guilt.

There were still sixteen or so hours a day that I was awake and had to manage. During the day when the girls were in school, I experienced some relief, but the weekends were very taxing. I was their main source of entertainment, along with Jen's mother. We did our best to keep them occupied and busy on the weekends with day trips, dinners out and other activities.

Then came a significant "first"—January 24th, Jen's birthday. For the days leading up to what would have been her 36th birthday, I mentally prepared myself for the pain. Like a tsunami scene in the 1998 movie, *Deep Impact*, I was sitting and knowing that a huge wave was going to be crashing on my shore, and there was nothing I could do to stop it.

January 24th came, and it turned into a day that all of us who loved her simply remembered her. It was not a day of celebration, but rather a day of contemplation.

I told Jen's parents that I did not want to celebrate her birthday, but rather just reflect. The girls went to day care, as they normally did, and I had four things I wanted to accomplish before the day was out. First, I visited Jen and tied a balloon to the handle of the vase that was affixed to her headstone. I wanted her to *know* I was there with her and remembering her on her birthday. I spent some time at the tomb, crying, and telling her how much I wished I could trade places with her. It was extremely therapeutic for me to cry uncontrollably at the cemetery. I never cared whether anyone was within an earshot; it was something I had to do, I realized, to give me the courage to go on.

After my time at the cemetery, I made my way down to our spot on the beach, in Avon-by-the-Sea. I purchased a second balloon and walked to the spot we always visited with the girls. I spoke to Jen for a minute, and then released the balloon. As the balloon drifted above the choppy waters of the Atlantic and farther away from me and harder to see from my vantage point, I videotaped it.

I returned to the stairs that led away from the boardwalk and down toward the sand. I had made a small 3" long x 2" wide laminated sign that read: IN LOVING MEMORY OF JENNIFER BALDASSARRE, HER STAIRCASE TO HEAVEN. It would temporarily serve as a remembrance of Jen until I received the more permanent plaque for placement on one of the many benches on the Avon boardwalk.

I stapled the small sign as best as I could to the side of the wooden staircase and kissed the palm of my hand

and then touched the sign as I sat in the sand. I was overcome by a surreal feeling, yet two things were very clear: 1) Jen was with me, even though I could not see her, and 2) she would have done the same for me.

I made my way home from the beach and completed the last of the remembrances to honor Jen. I made chicken pepperoni, her favorite birthday dinner and the traditional dish we cooked each year on her birthday. We had found the recipe in one of her cookbooks, and, coincidentally, it was featured in a movie we watched together, *Seems Like Old Times* with Chevy Chase and Goldie Hawn. The recipe was the cornerstone of the comedic conclusion of the movie.

I knew that I was going to be the only one who ate the chicken pepperoni, but I did not care. I was not about to interrupt the ritual we'd started when we moved to New Jersey. Discontinuing it would not have felt right. Even worse, if I did away with customs we cherished, Jen would begin to drift away from me— away from my soul, my heart, and, most importantly, my mind. Still to this day have a tremendous fear that I will forget those little quirks surrounding the special moments we shared and came to love about our time together. Furthermore, I felt that I had an obligation to the girls to continue these special things they lovingly associated with their mother.

That night in our house, though, there was no birthday cake, and everything was very subdued. The girls, their grandmother and I felt the void. The emotional scars ran deep that day for all of us. It was a day we simply had to acknowledge, not celebrate in joy. There was, however, one thing to celebrate. We had overcome the true first of firsts.

9

Hitting Rock-bottom

In fact, there were going to be many more firsts. Jen's birthday was over, but whether I knew it or not, my worst times were still lurking on the horizon. This is part of the journey. It is important to feel the pain so that you can still feel the love. The emotional tsunami was building up momentum and speed, and it was going to crash onto my shores in a big way; and in a manner that I was not expecting.

That's why this chapter was extremely difficult to write and why it was hard to be open and honest about what was happening and how I dealt with my pain. It is very important to stress that the specific sequence of events that transpire in this chapter revolving around my mental health are NO LONGER issues for me. I strongly encourage anyone who has similar problems to seek immediate help and hope that my words help anyone who is reading this book.

January ended in an unusually cold spell for New Jersey. I had made it through Jen's birthday, which was a triumph for me, but the feelings of dread and hopelessness began to escalate. With the end of the month approaching, I was nearing the end of health insurance coverage with my former employer. The girls and I still had time to make sure that we were going to be seen by all of our doctors and the dentist before February 1st. I investigated getting us enrolled in Medicaid. I knew that Rossella and Giada would be approved for coverage, but I was not sure about me.

After going through what I assumed was the typical phone screening with the New Jersey Medicaid provider, the girls and I were approved. Surprisingly, right then, I felt as if I had somehow failed as a parent. I was unable to provide my daughters medical coverage on my own. This was a fundamental, something I had always done either through my own employer or in concert with Jen's plan. As far as I was concerned, this was an indisputable failure, though others were telling me my ability to hold it together was a tremendous feat.

At the same time, I was well aware I needed a job. I had to have income coming in. I had built up a wealth of knowledge about compliance for addiction treatment providers over the past nine years. This led several friends to suggest I become a consultant and work on my own to assist treatment centers through the licensure and accreditation process and also helping them write or rewrite their standard operating procedures. Not a lot of people had the patience, let alone the understanding of what goes into behavioral health compliance, so even I had to agree this seemed like the perfect niche.

Before the end of January, I created my own

company, Baldassarre Consulting, LLC. Its mission was to provide the necessary support for addiction treatment providers. This new venture would bring some money in for me and the girls, and I was working in the field I enjoyed. In addition, it allowed me the flexibility of working my own hours while taking care of the girls and tending to my own needs.

At the same time, friends and family members were keeping in constant contact with me, checking up on me to make sure I was okay, and that the girls were doing as well as could be expected. Despite this support, I felt completely alone. I felt no one truly understood my pain.

I went to my primary care doctor to ask for help. I knew I needed medication, but I wasn't sure what type. My days were overwhelming and enormously trying, both physically and emotionally. My body simply wanted to shut down, and some days I did not want to get out of bed or move at all. My grief was paralyzing. I found myself just wanting to lie on the couch when the girls were in school and do nothing. Many afternoons I fell asleep because I was so upset and crying so much that it left me physically exhausted. I did not think it was humanly possible for me to experience pain like this. I had to be really in tune with how much I was able to do and take care not to physically push myself beyond those limits.

Jen's mother went home to Virginia at the beginning of February for some scheduled routine doctor appointments. She still had her life to live with Jen's father, and I wanted both of Jen's parents to have time together so that they could help each other through their grief. Everyone has a different way of grieving, and this is something I had come to respect over the months since Jen's death. Jen's mother felt that being with her granddaughters and helping me was her way of coping with Jen's loss. There was absolutely no judgment on my part; for all of us, it was about trying to survive.

In the days leading up to my mother-in-law's leave-taking, I had to mentally prepare myself for the fact that I was going to be on my own for a couple of weeks. I knew that I would be on deck to get the girls ready for school in the morning, cook dinner, bathe both girls, and put them to bed every night. I also realized that I was going to be alone, and I was petrified something might happen to me. What if my heart stopped just like Jen's, and I collapsed in the house when the girls were home? How would my daughters get help? If it happened at night, how would they even get out of the house, because I had a deadbolt on the front door that was out of their reach.

So, there were a few things that I implemented right away when Jen's mother went home. First, I began to leave the deadbolt on the front door unlocked whenever I was alone with the girls. I obviously knew that if there was an emergency, Rossella and Giada had to be able to get out of the house and get help. I told them to run across the street to Josh and Nicole's house, just like on the night that Mommy got sick. This was scary for me, but I had no choice but to instruct them to do so.

Second, I got into the practice of texting Josh and Nicole every night before I went to sleep so that they knew I was safe. This was simply an extra layer of security that provided comfort. I just needed someone to know that we were all safe and sound in our house.

Third, on the house phone, the same phone I used to call 911 the night that Jen went into cardiac arrest, I placed different color starts on the Talk, 9 and 1 buttons. I educated my daughters on several occasions on the sequence of buttons to press in case they ever had to call for help.

With all these precautions in place, I still felt anxious and scared. My grief continued to cripple me into early February. There were some days that the survivor's guilt consumed my daily sense of well-being. I could not reconcile being left behind, living, taking care of the girls without Jen. The pain and the sorrow—and the anger—were mounting inside of me. It reached a critical point when I felt that maybe I was never going to get better. These were feelings that were absolutely difficult to describe on paper—they were feelings I never before felt in my life.

On February 8th, 2018, I sat down at my home computer, when my daughters where in day care, and typed out my goodbye letter. I printed a copy and stored it in my home safe, along with my other important documents. I shared in my letter that the pain and suffering I was experiencing was too much for me to handle anymore; that the world had given me too much hardship and affliction. I felt that it would be less painful to be with Jen than to live on with my grief. In my mind, I did have a plan for executing my exit, and for two days I held onto the letter and envisioned the way I would leave this world.

I did speak to a few of my closest friends during

these two days and told them what I did, and they all stopped to tell me that it was the wrong thing to do for so many reasons: the selfishness of depriving the girls of both of their parents, the high probability that I would not see Jen if I crossed over, the fact that so many people genuinely cared for the girls and me. These were people who would stick by my side through thick and thin.

These were all factors that pulled me out of the emotional abyss in which I'd been drowning and set me on a more responsible route. I brought a copy of the letter to my therapist, who assessed whether for my safety I required hospitalization. After a review of my protective and risk factors, she determined that it would be better for my girls to have their father at home rather than in the hospital. She made me sign a safety contract, and thanks to the help of my support network, the feelings of bleakness and misery subsided. On February 10th, I ripped up the letter. I even took a picture of it and sent it to my therapist and those friends with whom I had shared my intentions during the last two days. Needless to say, everyone was greatly relieved when they knew the letter was gone.

But most importantly, ripping up the letter was for Jen. I had gone down to the boardwalk in Avon-by-the-Sea to rip up that letter so Jen could witness this action. Then, I asked for her forgiveness.

10

Time Loss

Throughout the early months of 2018, I was obsessed with watching the 1990's TV show, the *X-Files*. I guess it was the escape from reality that provided me with some much-needed relief. In a strange way, watching episodes about suspected vampires, monsters, and alien abductions comforted me. I would record a bunch of episodes on my DVR and watch them while the girls were in school or after they would go to bed.

In a couple of episodes, Agent Fox Mulder explained his theory of "time loss," in which alien abductees would experience an unexplainable loss of time from the moment they were physically abducted until the time they were returned to earth. In one episode, Agents Scully and Mulder were driving down a typical rain swept, foggy road somewhere in Oregon, when they were abducted by a UFO. The abduction took place during a nine-minute stretch during which neither Scully or Mulder could remember what had occurred. But they both knew that they were "gone" for those nine minutes because their wrist watches were nine minutes behind the clock in the car.

When I saw this episode of the *X-Files*, my first thought was, *Wow, this is a great plot.* Then my mind immediately jumped to the thought, *Oh my God, that's me in a way. I experienced time loss.* To be more exact, I would have moments in which I would lose complete sense to time with no recollection of what I just did—not even remember how I got to that point. This commonly happened while I was driving; I would realize how much time lapsed, and I would have no way of recollecting my thoughts, even when I tried to remember what I had just done.

I was getting extremely upset with myself for the frequency of my time loss, because it was a tangible sign that I was experiencing extreme anxiety and stress. When I was younger, I had a great memory and was able to recall an incredible amount of facts and figures, especially telephone numbers. I was now at a point in my life where I could not remember which roads to take home. I could not drive from Point A to Point B without getting completely lost, questioning where I was, and how I got there. I had lived in Howell for three years at that point, eight years in Monmouth County. I knew every road between the shore points and my house, but now all of it presented a unique and frustrating challenge.

There was one exception to my time loss: I always remembered the way to Jen's resting place. I had discovered every possible route to the cemetery, from Interstate 195, from Route 34, from Route 35, the

Garden State Parkway, and all the backroads that did not require me to get on a major highway. During those rides, I was alert. I regained my sense of direction. I knew how I got from Point A to Point B. Even if it was just for a little while, it was as if I had found the cure for time loss, and in those moments, I felt comforted.

Eventually, my bouts of time loss became less severe and less frequent, but every now and then I find myself questioning what I did with the time leading up to those lost moments. I know there were not little green men beaming me up in their ships, but on occasion I still find myself on a road and don't remember how I got there— don't remember how to get to my Point B.

With the help of my support group, I would eventually learn, that I would have to cut myself some slack—in some cases, a lot of slack. I would need to go easy on myself and try to pick up the pieces when I could. No one is perfect and the road to recovery may be a long and arduous journey. It was a journey I did not want to make, but it's what would be required.

The Necessities for Survival

My friend Jenna is a licensed clinical social worker in the state of New Jersey. I had worked with her, and we stayed in close contact. She had come to Jen's wake and was supportive as I struggled with my grief in the aftermath of Jen's death. I valued her opinion, because she had many years of experience in providing insight and counseling to others. She also had two small children and was married to a police officer in a neighboring town, so she could understand how devastating it was to lose your partner.

When I considered ending my life, I confided in her. She helped me connect with the appropriate mental health providers. She also acted as a sounding board.

She was aware that I hit rock-bottom in February 2018, and her instincts took over. She knew the girls needed their father and was dedicated to stabilizing my mental health. She realized that I needed more than just individual therapy. My therapist was great and did a tremendous job helping me, but sometimes the bleeding needed to be controlled with a bigger bandage. The grief and trauma were so powerful that sometimes I continued to find myself helpless in face of their power over me. I believed that unless someone had suffered the same loss as I had, they would not be able to comprehend the magnitude of the pain and suffering that a survivor experiences.

I had no qualms telling people what happened on that night back in November, or in the 19 days that followed. But when I would tell people how I felt during that time, everyone pretty much had the same response: "I don't know what to say."

I had grown accustomed to responding: "There is nothing to say." And of course, everyone would be incredibly sympathetic and would try to understand.

The problem was that I found myself having this conversation almost daily. It had become tiresome to me. Was there anyone who could understand the way I was feeling? My friends and family were deeply concerned and cared about Giada, Rossella and me, but this was simply not enough. When Jenna saw my frustration, she suggested I attend a meeting at the center that offered free support groups for people who had lost a loved one. It was a support center entirely devoted to grief and loss. At one time, Jenna had provided clinical supervision to the woman who ran the program and encouraged me to give it a try.

I will admit, my initial thought of talking about what had happened to Jen and how this affected to our family and me in the months that followed her death was unsettling. I did not know any of the people that would be in the support group, but Jenna said—and Dennis, Josh, and Nicole agreed—would be comforting to share with individuals who *understood* what it meant to lose a spouse, especially at a young age with children. What sold me was the fact that I was going to be talking to people who had experienced a situation that was pretty much the carbon copy of what had happened to me. This group would provide me with a forum to discuss what was really troubling me. Most of all, it would give me people to lean on as I continued on my journey.

It was a bit surreal driving to my first support group. The group was in Red Bank, about twenty minutes from my house. It was inconceivable that I was going to be around people who had suffered a similar loss. The group was composed of widows and widowers between the ages of 25 and 45. Even the owner of the center and facilitator of the group had lost her husband in the World Trade Center during the September 11th attacks.

Walking into the center, I began to feel eerily comfortable. I knew I would be able to spill my guts about the hellish events that I had endured and not feel that I was making anyone uncomfortable. Most important to me, they would understand what it felt like to lose a life partner.

We started the group by reading an affirmation from a book that is geared specially toward widows and widowers. Then I had to introduce myself to the group by explaining how Jen passed away. I always tell people that even though Jen officially passed on December 11th, I consider her date of passing as the day she collapsed in the kitchen. I had to pause several times while I was retelling the story because I started to experience the feelings of that night all over again—the coldness of the kitchen tile on my skin, the noises of Jen gasping for air, and me trying to slide her on her side to prevent her from choking.

Finally, everyone shared their stories. Of the four women who were present that day, two of the women lost their husbands in car accidents. One widow lost her husband one month after Jen. Another woman lost her husband very suddenly the day after he was diagnosed with leukemia. Still another had lost her husband to cancer about 18 months prior.

It was upsetting to hear all the stories, one after another. Everyone was at a different stage of grief, which was oddly beneficial. We all had different perspectives, and all of the stories were equally tragic. No one could possibly say "I suffered more than you," or "At least, you had time with your partner before they died." Some people's stories included them fighting with their spouses right before they passed; some had no warning signs that it would be their last day with their partner. Some had kids who were grown and had moved out of the house, while some had young children who could not remember their parent who had passed away. My story was distinctive in its own way, but it was equally painful and filled with sorrow, just like the stories of everyone who was in that room with me. For the first time since Jen left me, I felt as though I was finally with people who actually understood how it felt to experience such a devastating loss, and how you are forced to pick up the pieces and move on, for yourself and for your kids.

I began to think of a young widow/widower assuming the role of a vice president who becomes president after an assassination, or in an instance in which the president dies suddenly while in office. This has happened many times in American history: Andrew Johnson in 1865 after Lincoln was shot; Theodore Roosevelt in 1901 when William McKinley was shot by an assassin; and Harry Truman in 1945 when Franklin Roosevelt unexpectedly died in office. However, the one instance that absolutely personifies this analogy was Lyndon Johnson, ascending to the Presidency in 1963 when John F. Kennedy was gunned down in Dallas.

JFK's untimely and tragic demise had eerie similarities for me. In a way, I felt like LBJ, a man stepping into a role who had to show everyone I was ready to take charge and continue on in the face of disaster. Nobody told LBJ that on November 22, 1963—the exact day that Jen collapsed but 44 years later—he would become President of the United States and bring the people together to heal a nation following the death of the President from an assassin's bullet. LBJ had to go on, conducting the business of the nation, being strong for all of those looking to him for guidance, direction, and most importantly, the strength people so desperately needed at that time.

In my case, I suddenly found myself a widower and a single parent of four-year old twin daughters. I had to find—perhaps create—meaning in a world that had lost all significance when Jen took her last labored breath in hospice. The world had completely changed, and certainly not for the better. I began to believe that many people—my family, friends, Jen's co-workers, and even people who did not know me before Jen's death—looked at me as someone who was a role model for what to do after losing a spouse. Sometimes, I felt as if I was under a huge magnifying glass, having every move criticized by dozens of people, intentionally or unintentionally. I felt that it was necessary to put on a great façade for everyone. "Look at how great he has it together." That's what I thought everyone was thinking when instead I thought it was a sham. I was completely under water, barely able to keep up with the daily routines of life.

Over time, though, with the insight and support of the other widows and widowers, I slowly began to see that it did not matter what others thought or would think. In fact, I came to realize that it was absolutely counterproductive to let the thoughts and concerns of others influence how I was coping with Jen's death.

Sitting in the first few widows' groups, it became clear to me that if I were to take everyone's advice and opinions about what to do in the weeks and months that followed Jen's death, it would have created nothing but chaos. I would just be spinning my wheels in the mud.

I knew physically and mentally that I was doing everything that I could for Giada and Rossella. Why, then, did it matter what others thought about me, as long as the girls' needs were addressed? What's more, I was essentially parenting the same way as I would have if Jen had not died, so there was really no difference.

Finally, and probably one the most important things I realized almost immediately: If there is categorically no way to satisfy everyone, even if I wanted to, why would or should I even try? Why waste so much mental energy and strength on other people when my energy could be devoted to my daughters and my self-care? I had to be happy with myself and the decisions I made in order for me to survive. That's what it all came down to: survival.

I started to feel more connected with the participants in my support group. Over the course of several weeks in the winter and spring of 2018, I got to meet all the group participants, hear their stories and feel their individual pain.

Whether widows or widowers, their grief was distinctive and extraordinary, and they all had their own way of coming to grips with their loss. Some only went to this support group, while others had additional means of support, including individual therapy and medication. It did not matter to any of us where you were on your journey or how you were coping with your loss, or even if you moved on to dating again. We all shared a bond, a reason that unfortunately brought us all together, and we were going to be there for one another. This connection was what I needed. Finally, I was finding some emotional security and comfort.

At the end of each group meeting, everyone would hold hands and recite the Serenity prayer together:

**God grant me the Serenity to accept the things I cannot change,
The courage to change the things I can and the wisdom to know the difference.**

I would recite this prayer with the people in my group and they would become some of my dearest friends. But deep down it would not feel appropriate to acknowledge God. Theological debates notwithstanding, I was angry with God. Why should God, if he/she does exist, help me at this point, after I had lost so much?

To this day, I sincerely want God to give me some concrete reason for ending Jen's life at 35? Why did my daughters have to witness their mother dying? What purpose did any of this serve in the grand scheme of life? None of this made any sense to me. There were individuals who time and again would say to me, "It's all part of the plan." Honestly, this pissed me off. I cried "bullshit," even when I recited the Serenity.

Over time, however, with the guidance of my support group, this anger and resentment receded. I came to understand that if believing in a Higher Power comforted people, then good for them. Believing in God was not a comfort to me. God was not part of *my* solution. Yet I could respect the fact other people found solace in that belief and were comforted knowing that someone or something was watching over them in their time of need. But I knew then as I know now that this intangible that is God was not and is not going to help me in my recovery. I yearned for tangible items to make me feel better; items and actions that I could see for myself to help me heal and move on.

Everyone manages grief and loss differently, and in my world, God does not have to be part of that process.

Still, there is no instruction manual that tells people how to grieve. There is no right or wrong way. The important thing is that you allow yourself to grieve. It is only when you fully experience your grief that you can learn to stand tall in the world again.

12

Music Soothes the Soul

I was getting friendlier with the people in my support group, but I was still eagerly looking for new ways to help myself relax. There were still some nights that I had a couple of drinks to help me wind down, but never to the point that I was not able to take care of the girls. Some nights I forced myself to watch funny YouTube videos, mainly clips of Robin Williams' standup or Bill Maher's *Real Time*. I will admit: the alcohol and the comedy were a good mix, but I knew this was not a viable, long-term solution.

A friend in the support group told me how much she relied on music to take her out of her sadness after her husband died. She was a big fan of all types of music, but country music was her absolute favorite. A music aficionado, she knew almost every song that was on the radio, as well as every song that had been out for the last 25 or so years; not just country music, though that was truly her favorite.

When Jen was alive, I was never a big music fan, though I did enjoy listening to music from the 1980's. I even listened to a lot of oldies too, but what my friend started to show me was completely different.

Music can heal and soothe the soul, she said, when grief and sadness become all consuming. She suggested I turn to music for support whenever I needed to and shared some of her favorite songs with me and even showed me the playlists on her iPhone. What intrigued me about her playlist selection was that she had created different playlists to achieve different moods— for empowerment when she faced a challenged, consolation when her grief was overbearing, or, simply for a quick pick-me-up when she just wanted to feel better.

I began to listen to the radio more carefully, taking note of which songs made me feel better, ones that really made me smile or even took my mind off Jen. I then made sure that these songs made their way into my IPhone under a playlist titled "Pick Me Up." Even if I added one song a week to my playlist, if the song had a positive effect on my overall well-being, then I downloaded it onto my cell phone.

Ironically, and very fortunate for me, the first two songs that made their way onto my playlist were "I Won't Back Down," by Tom Petty and "Stand" by R.E.M. These two songs had special meaning for me. They emboldened me to drive forward and realize that no matter how crappy life got for me, I had to be stronger, especially for my daughters, and I had to have as many tools as possible available at my disposal to achieve this.

The third song on my cell phone was "Sunshine on My Shoulders" by John Denver. I put it on my playlist because I like the song and it is uplifting. Even more important, a medium told me that she was singing this song to me whenever she is with me, trying to make me feel better. I played this song whenever tears came. It was something tangible that strengthened my bond with Jen.

13

Come and Talk with Me, Jen

A few of my support group friends regularly visited a local medium to talk to their loved ones. I never believed in people having the ability to talk to others who were no longer in this world. I thought I knew how people worked this scam. They researched what they could about you and your loved ones on the internet and brought that information to the session with them. Then, using yes or no questions and reasonable deduction, they compiled a somewhat accurate profile of statements and facts that would make the person going for the reading believe they were really speaking to a loved one who had died.

My friends firmly believed that the psychic was legitimate. Still, they recommended following three important rules during visits: 1) Do not provide your last name for whatever reason; 2) Do not provide information to the psychic unless it is required because you could essentially be providing information that could make it seem that they are talking to the deceased when actually they are not; and 3) Ask open ended questions. With yes and no questions, there is always a 50/50 chance that the medium will guess the right answer.

So, I decided to schedule an appointment. This medium was someone who was well-respected in New Jersey. She had assisted local police departments on a few cases. She had also given readings several months prior to my friends in the support group.

To make the appointment, I had to text her assistant because the psychic's voice mailbox was full. It took about a week for her assistant to call me back, and I made an hour-long appointment for a Sunday morning. I was pleased I made the appointment, because I felt going to a medium was a rite of passage for a widower. Plus, it put me on the same path with others in my group.

My appointment was not for four weeks, and as the day of appointment grew closer, my anxiety began to build. By the fourth week, I was noticeably uneasy and worried that I was going to unintentionally feed the medium information about Jen and me—even worse, that Jen would not be reached so that I would have no communication with her at all.

The night before my appointment I went to Jen's grave. I approached her marble headstone and told her flat out, "You better come and speak to me tomorrow morning." I logically knew I was only speaking to a slab of marble, but it was necessary for me to do this before I went seeing the medium the next morning. As I left the cemetery that evening, I found myself hoping and praying again—this time, to somehow talk to Jen again.

When I arrived at the medium, I first took note of how unelaborate her office suite was; it just had a big folding table, and oversized leather chairs, one for her and one for me. The medium also had some blank paper for her to write on during the session, in case she had to write specific notes. Other than that, the room was empty.

As we began the session, the medium told me there were a lot of spirits surrounding me: the two that immediately jumped out were my mother, and my maternal grandmother who had succumbed to heart failure in 1996. Both spirits told the medium that they were proud of the way I had handled the events of the last few months and assured me they were continuously trying to provide me with support and strength. They also told me they were sending me signs to show that they were always with me—the strongest sign being my mother directing me to find pennies on the ground.

About ten or fifteen minutes into my session, my grandmother and mother turned the session over to Jen, and I immediately began to cry. This was the moment I had been waiting for. Skeptics have said to me, "Joe, how do you know that Jen was even there?" The next forty-five minutes would have turned any skeptic into a believer.

One of the first things Jen told the medium was that she was sorry. She said she did not believe she was going to die but rather that it was all a bad dream. I guess reality struck when she crossed over and my mother was the first one to greet her and take her under her wing. Jen informed the medium too that she was free of pain and able to breathe. The medium asked me if Jen had died unexpectedly and whether she had died at our house. She also specifically asked if Jen's heart had stopped beating.

Jen told the medium several key facts: 1) the medium was truly speaking to Jen and 2) more importantly, that Jen watches over and is always with the girls and me.

In April 2018, I took the girls, our neighbors, Josh and Nicole, and their daughter to an indoor water park in the Pocono Mountains in Pennsylvania for two nights. I did not say a word to the medium about this trip. Yet the medium said that Jen was at the indoor water park with us. The internet notwithstanding, there was simply no way the medium could have known this.

Something else validated that the medium was in contact with Jen. I was at one of my lowest points on New Year's Eve 2017. Still numb from the funeral and basically an emotional time bomb, I got upset with both girls because they were out of control and fighting and hitting one another. I took one of their tablets and smashed it on the floor. Surely, this was not my finest moment as a person, let alone a parent. The medium told me that Jen was there when this incident happened. What's more, this was one of the only times since Jen had died that she was honestly upset with my behavior. There was simply no way the medium could have known this story.

Something else that the psychic said resonated with me. She said Jen was attempting to speak to me by focusing her energy and spirit through electronics, specifically my cell phone. The medium told me that Jen had recently been messing with my cell phone. Amazingly, in the days leading up to my appointment, my cell phone was not charging while it was on the charger. I tried multiple chargers around the house and none of the chargers worked. This had never happened to me before, and there was no rhyme or reason why this was happening now.

Toward the end of the session, the medium told me that Jen was always in the car with me. On the drive home I reached my hand over to the passenger seat, trying to somehow hold Jen's hand—something I do to this day. Rossella and Giada always ask if mommy is in the passenger seat. My answer is always "of course."

The medium shared a few more things about Jen watching over me. She usually comes in the middle of the night between 2 a.m. and 3 a.m. Apparently, this is the time when her energy is the strongest. Jen also is always praying for me and trying to give me the strength to get through each day. And, finally, of course, Jen is with our cat, Anastasia, who passed away one month before Jen collapsed. I figured this even before I saw the medium.

When the session was over, I was in complete awe, mesmerized by the depth, scope and detail of the medium's references to Jen. I made it into my car, closed the car door, and cried for fifteen minutes straight. I was unable to drive because I was thrilled I got to speak to Jen again but upset by the fact this was the only way I could communicate with her. One thing, though. At least from what I could tell, Jen had begun to cross over, and she seemed accepting and at peace.

During the ride home, I envisioned Jen sitting in the passenger seat, trying her best to give me a sign, telling me that she was with me. Right then, though, I did not need the sign because I now knew in my heart that she was with me and the girls all the time.

That night, after the girls settled down and fell asleep, I decided to lay in bed, put on my earbuds, and listen to the entire one-hour session again. I had recorded it in its entirety on my cell phone. I was compelled to do so because I wanted to fully absorb everything that the medium had told me and burn it into my memory, which seemed to have broken down since Jen died. This was a chance for me to slowly begin to rebuild my mind by focusing on something that was critical for me to remember and retain so that I could call it up when I needed comfort.

There have been plenty of times that I have looked over on the other side of the bed, or across the dinner table, or even on the side of the couch next to me and known that Jen is there. She would never allow her spirit to leave us in our most difficult time. I do not view her as my guardian angel. I will always view her as the love of my life—the love who will never leave my side and will continue to support the girls and me not only through our grief but also throughout our lives.

The experience with the medium provided me with comfort that helps me to function day-to-day. Bottom line: As long as it's healthy, I will do anything I can do to get through the day. It's not a question of whether or not I believe in something; it's having something in which to believe.

14

First Glimpse Beyond the Darkness

February was coming to a close, and the winter seemed like it never wanted to end. As March began, it remained cold and snowy. This was the first year that I honestly thought I had enough with the snow and darkness of the early nights. I was looking forward to spring and having some type of outdoor fun again with my daughters. The light at the end of the tunnel was spending time on the beach in Avon-by-the-Sea. Jen had always started counting down the weeks until we were able to buy our season badges for the beach, and this year I was the one counting the weeks.

About this time, I received an invite to a St. Patrick's Day Party: "For the Love of the Leprechaun." The invite came from Terri, the mother of one of the kids in the girls' day care class, St. Patrick's Day was on a Saturday, which meant all of the parents would be celebrating in the typical holiday fashion—consuming as much alcohol as possible but doing so in a manner that still allowed them to care for their children. This was going to be the second time that I had been with the parents of the "Wolfpack" since Jen died (the first being two days before Jen's funeral), so I was looking forward to having somewhat of a break from everything. I had to come to learn if you had the chance to take a break, you took it. The girls were excited to spend time with their friends from school; they had been with them since they were a year old, and we all treated each other like family.

Terri, her husband Adam, and their son, Dylan, lived in Brick, which was only about fifteen minutes from our house. On the day of the party, I left my house a little earlier in case I got lost.

We were the first people to arrive, and I had some time to talk to Terri and Adam before the other guests arrived. They had been there for the girls and me right after Jen died; they attended Jen's funeral service, even though they had never met her in person. They looked at me, as most people have, as someone who was in tremendous pain. They admired my resilience and perseverance to go on despite the tremendous loss I had experienced. Most importantly, they did not view me as a widower, but just as Joe, a normal guy with two kids. This was one of the first times after Jen's death that I felt normal and I welcomed the feeling.

Gradually, the other parents and kids arrived, and to my delight, the girls jumped right in. While the girls were playing their friends, I was in the kitchen with the other parents. Everyone was decked out in green and had matching four-leaf clover paraphernalia. Within minutes, some parents asked me how the girls and I were doing. Others waited. My answer was always the same: "We are okay, just trying to find a way to survive and get through this one day at a time." I knew everyone in the house that evening cared deeply for the girls and me. It felt really good to be surrounded by all of these people who were looking out for us.

All of the parents were talking, laughing, and have a great time. Of course, the parents were drinking as well, as well keeping an eye on their kids. All the kids there had a mommy and a daddy. I was the only single parent present but I let my guard down enough to allow myself to have a little bit of fun and not get smothered by my feelings of loss. I knew that night that I was loving the girls for both of us. Rossella and Giada had only one living parent, but they were not loved any less.

The St. Patrick's Day party at Adam's and Terri's house was somewhat of a test for me: how would I allow myself to reconcile feelings of contentment and peace with my need to grieve and cope with my ongoing depression and lingering symptoms of post-traumatic stress disorder? These conflicting emotions were at war inside of me. How was I going to be able to enjoy any portion of my life wholeheartedly? How could I even think of being happy again? Was it even allowed? These were all questions that plagued me for months, as did any type of activity that gave me the opportunity to feel joy.

I came to learn this was survivors' guilt which by any stretch of the imagination is not out of the ordinary for a widows and widowers. Nevertheless, it is a horrible feeling. There were plenty of times I was consumed with guilt, wishing I was the one in the coffin. That choice, however, was not mine to make. Jen was gone, and there was nothing that could change that for me. I had to convince myself that I could have moments of happiness that provided a respite from my grief. My grief and the accompanying trauma from what I experienced was not only troubling but also draining on so many levels. The party on St. Patrick's Day was just that for me: a break from my bereavement.

In addition, I had to detach from all of the sadness and give myself permission to start living again. Admittedly, that proved to be more difficult than it sounds, but slowly I chiseled away at the notion that I was not allowed to have fun and enjoy life.

Overall, the party was beneficial to me in many ways. The girls obviously had a great evening and slept extremely well that night. I got to connect with my friends in a more enjoyable and cheerful setting. Most importantly, it provided me with my first litmus test of how a widower or widow could potentially start to pick up the pieces. If only for a few hours, the party allowed me to live again.

15

Reconstruction

When I first met the love of my life, we were both in the same 9th grade classes at Pocono Mountain High School. I had an instant crush on Jen, and I loved trying to do all of our school projects together, even though we were just friends.

One of the classes Jen and I had together was American History 1860-1990. Presidents Lincoln to Bush were covered in that school year. In that class, we learned about the Reconstruction era following the Civil War. It was fascinating to me how our nation had to rebuild itself in a variety of different ways after one of the most difficult times in its history. Our country was literally torn apart and had to put itself back together again.

Following the St. Patrick's Day party at Adam and Terri's house, I realized I was in the midst of a Reconstruction myself. I experienced something that literally destroyed the way I had lived my life. Now, I was forced to find and use all the resources at my disposal to rebuild my life into something totally different. As one of my friends from support group said: "The old you died when your spouse died, and that person is never coming back." Neither was my life.

What was my new life without Jen going to look like? Immediately, I knew of a few things I had to take care of and made some decisions that were going to affect the way I lived my life, at least in the short term.

My first objective was to get my finances in order. I relied heavily on my financial planner at Morgan Stanley, and I trusted him immensely. He came to Jen's wake, and I had been in constant communication with him since her funeral. I had to make sure all of the financial decisions I was making from here on out were going to provide a much-needed safety net for Rossella, Giada, and me. My advisor created a portfolio that allowed my funds to be properly invested and created income to live on until my employment situation stabilized.

I also opened 529 college savings plan accounts for both girls, so I could begin to save money for their college educations. These plans and the monthly survivor benefits the girls were receiving from Social Security would help to secure the future for them and provide them with the resources to achieve their goals, whatever they may be.

I also made the decision that at least for the remainder for 2018, I would only work as a consultant through my LLC, providing services to new, as well as existing, addiction treatment providers. Having work flexibility would ensure that I would be present for the girls as they transitioned from day care to kindergarten. This was the first time since I graduated from college in

2005 that I was not going to work full time, and I knew that this was going to be an adjustment. Still, I knew this was the right thing to do, because my priority was the girls' well-being—my priority was being there for them.

Next, I turned my attention to the girls' social, emotional and medical needs. Giada and Rossella and had suffered a devastating loss. Plus, they had been here when Jen collapsed in the kitchen that day. I had no way of knowing how much all this affected them emotionally. Did they have a lot of pent up anger and resentment? Were they depressed or even despondent? Or was there more to their feelings that I was not seeing? After all, they were only four-years old, and from a developmental standpoint they were not able to fully describe how they felt. As their therapist told me during one of their sessions, sometimes children are not able to fully articulate their feelings. If not properly addressed now, this would present challenges later on.

Some people believed that the girls should have started therapy sooner, around the time I did. My feeling, however, was that I had to get to a strong enough place myself to be in a position to help them. My thinking echoed the popular dictum to put on your oxygen mask before helping others, particularly your children, in an airplane emergency. The concept was the same in the grieving process. Some people may have disagreed, but at the end of the day it did not matter what they thought, because I knew I was doing what was the best for all of us.

I also made it a point to make sure that the girls were not left out of any social activities, and that they had plenty of friends and family surrounding them in their lives. I set them up with as many play dates as possible with their friends from school, as well as with their cousins. Indeed, these play days made them very happy.

The girls had only me now, but it was crucial that they still reaped the benefits of their mother's love. I was the one who best understood how Jen wanted to parent Giada and Rossella, and it was vital that her presence, her desires, and most of all, her love for them was very real for them. Many people have told me that the girls are lucky to have me as their father, but my response is always the same: "I always do what any loving parent would do for them, especially Jen."

16

A Setback in the Summer

In New Jersey most of the beaches require people over 12 years old to pay a fee to access the beach. People can buy daily passes, which are required if people want to access the beach between 9 a.m. and 5 p.m. Most locals, however, purchase season badges which more or less pay for themselves in about ten visits. Since our first summer at the Jersey Shore, Jen and I always purchased season badges for ourselves, even during the summer of 2013 when she was pregnant with the twins. We usually rushed to purchase our badges for Avon-by-the-Sea the first week in May when the town puts them on sale. In 2018, I did not want it to be any different, so I bought two badges even though I knew our beachgoing routine would be different this year.

The beach was still a place full of wonderful memories, but I was not ready to fully embrace being at the beach without Jen. It was a difficult place for me to physically be without her, whether I was in Avon or at any other beach, so I knew that I was not going to take the girls to the beach as much as Jen and I had taken them during the previous summers.

As summer kicked off, and the temperatures rose, the girls and I did make our way to the shore. The girls loved running to and from the water, burying their dolls in the sand and watching the planes fly by along the coastline with advertisement banners draped behind them.

Concurrently, the girls transitioned to their final classroom in day care before they officially became kindergarteners. They went to day care Monday through Friday and enjoyed being with the friends they made since they enrolled in the school in 2014.

On Thursday, June 28th, I was on my way to pick the girls up from day care, travelling south on the Garden State Parkway, when I received a phone call from the day care director: "Rossella tripped and fell on the playground, and she is not able to walk," the director said. This was a phone call that no parent wants to receive from their child's school.

I vividly remember that after I hung up with the day care, I said out loud in the car: "I don't f***ing need this. Damn you, Jen, for leaving me." I quickly realized what I said, apologized to Jen by looking towards the seat next to me, and said, "I'm sorry sweetheart." I then picked up speed and made my way to the school.

When I arrived at the day care center, Rossella was in the director's office with Giada, and one other teacher. Her left leg was bent at the knee, and she was unable to put any weight on it, even to limp. I knew as soon as I saw her that she needed to go to the emergency room. I scooped her up and took her to my car. Jen's parents were picking up Giada. Going to the nearest hospital meant that I would again be at hospital Jen was taken to the night she collapsed.

The hospital was only a five-minute drive from the day care center. When I arrived, I decided to use the valet service that was free to visitors because the front entrance was a short walk from the car.

Thankfully, we entered the hospital through an entrance different from the one I had used the night of Jen's collapse. The triage area was different, too. As soon as we were admitted, Rossella was whisked away to a special pediatric center.

Within minutes of getting situated in her room, Rossella's doctor came in for a brief examination, followed by two nurses who took an X-ray of her leg to determine if it was fractured or just sprained. Rossella was scared, but she was trying to understand to the best of her ability what was going to happen next.

X-rays were taken and saved electronically for the doctor to review. As Rossella was lying on the bed, I turned on the television to distract her from what was happening. It worked because, as always, her attention was focused solely on the colorful cartoons in front of her.

Sure enough, my worst fear had been verified by the physician. Rossella had fractured her tibia bone and was going to require a hard cast for a few weeks. To me, this was the equivalent of getting my face kicked in after someone had landed a knockout punch on me. Questions started running through my mind: "What did

I do in life to deserve any of this?" Was this a karmic experiment to test my endurance and strength as an individual?

I called Jen's parents who were back at the house with Giada to update them. Of course, they were surprised and taken aback by the news. How was it even possible that a four-year old could break her tibia bone in such a bad way? Regardless, this type of occurrence was going to be, at least for the short term, the new reality of my life.

The hospital wrapped up Rossella's leg in an elastic bandage and discharged her just two hours after she was admitted to the hospital. I was given the name of a local pediatric orthopedist and told to follow up with him so that she could be given a hard cast.

When we got home, I carried Rossella into the house and placed her on the living room couch so that she could lie down and watch television. Giada, at first, was anxious to see her sister, scared even to see the bandaged leg. She wanted reassurance that her sister was going to be okay (Giada knew what had happened the last time someone in her household went to the hospital). Giada grew more and more frightened about Rossella's injury and did not even want to look at Rossella's leg; I had to keep a blanket draped over it to quell Giada's fears.

For the next three days, Rossella did not move off of my bed or the living room couch. She required someone to carry her to the bathroom and situate her on the toilet. All of her food had to be carried to her directly to her, and she had to be dressed and undressed with someone's help.

The weekend before she was placed in the hard cast, the three of us attended my father's family's previously scheduled pool party. Unfortunately, Rossella was not able to play in the pool and was forced to remain indoors while most of the other guests enjoyed the water in the near 100-degree heat. Rossella was miserable during the party, but my family and I did the best we could to keep her occupied and happy during the party.

When she received the cast that Monday, July 2nd, it was a sigh of relief for me, as I took that as a sign that she was just a little bit closer to recovering from injury. Jen's father and I drove Rossella to her appointment with the orthopedic pediatrician in Brick. I had developed a system to make Rossella comfortable and safe in the car and placed the back of the front passenger seat all the way down to where it was as flat as it could be so she could prop up her broken leg, resting it on a pillow so that it could be as elevated and cushioned as possible.

I was forced to carry her into the doctor's waiting room and then again into the examination room. In order to safely carry her, I had to cradle Rossella in my arms, as if she were an infant. She was too big and too heavy, especially with the cast, to pick her straight up in front of me as if I were giving her a hug.

As we were waiting for the doctor to come in, Rossella was telling me and her grandfather that she was scared because she thought she was going to get a shot. I did not want to give her any additional fears about going to a doctor because of what had happened with Jen. In no way did I want either of the girls to develop unnecessary anxiety about seeing doctors and other medical professionals. Thankfully, this never happened.

When the doctor came into the room, he reviewed

the X-rays that were taken at the hospital and concluded that she needed to be placed in a hard cast for four weeks, from just below her waist down to her foot. In addition, the cast could not get wet at all (keep in mind this was the beginning of July and both of my daughters loved the water). Additionally, and pardon the pun, but to add insult to injury, Rossella was too young to receive crutches, so she would either have to be given a pediatric wheelchair or have to be carried everywhere she went for the next month. The doctor explained that by the time Rossella would have learned to use the crutches properly and developed the necessary stamina to walk with them, it would be time for the cast to be removed. So, essentially, this meant that my daughter was temporarily immobile, and would need to rely on other people to get her around for the short term.

Rossella chose to have her cast set in pink. This was her favorite color, and she was happy to see that it was not going to be plain white. Two nurses carefully wrapped her leg up in clean bandages, followed by the pink plaster. Rossella was forced to position her leg in a fashion as to ensure that her leg would properly heal without further injury. To say the least, this was uncomfortable and prompted tears. Her cries cut through me like a knife. I attempted to distract her by playing one of her favorite cartoons, Peppa Pig, on my cell phone, but this was not enough to get her mind off what was happening. She continued to scream, terrified of the pain she anticipated, especially when the cast became harder and heavier. The plaster dried quickly, and we were allowed to leave. She was given a follow up appointment for two weeks from that day, and we were on our way home.

When we arrived home, I called the day care center owner and told her of Rossella's diagnosis and her expected length of recovery. This was when I was handed yet another blow. Rossella was not permitted back at day care until her cast came off and she was able to walk on her own again. This was essential because going to the restroom and, if necessary, evacuating the building during an emergency, would be virtually impossible. Getting her a wheelchair was not an option either, because she needed to learn how to use the toilet on her own, without the help of any of the day care staff. So, what did this all mean for me? Simply put, Rossella would remain home with me for the duration of the time that she had her cast on her leg.

To further complicate matters, I was already going to be on my own, with the two girls without the assistance of Jen's mother, from July 4th to August 2nd. Jen's mother had to go back home to Virginia for previously scheduled doctors' appointments. She offered to postpone them, but as I told her, I needed her to be healthy for the girls and for her husband, so it would not make any sense for her to reschedule the appointments. Everyone's health and well-being were paramount at this point for both Rossella and Giada, and they did not need to endure any other family members getting sick or hurt.

My mind immediately went into operational mode when I realized what was lying ahead for me. Four weeks, going solo, with one child who was essentially disabled. I had therapy sessions, as well as my weekly support group to attend, so I needed to find people who were willing to watch Rossella at home while I ran to my appointments. Giada was at this time still going to day care without her sister, so she also needed to be dropped off and picked up.

In addition, there was still the issue of getting Rossella around the house. She needed to be lifted to and from the toilet, to and from the kitchen, and to and from her bed. Even if she wanted a snack from the kitchen, it required me, or whoever was watching her, to get it for her and carry it over to her on the couch. My life for four weeks was going to strictly revolve around attending to the specific needs of Rossella.

The realization of not having a second parent around to assist with all these tasks really hit me hard. Jen and I would have been coordinating our schedules, taking turns lifting Rossella around the house, and splitting our time appropriately between the two girls. I was all on my own now. Everything fell on me.

Luckily, I made some phone calls to our friends who lived in the immediate area. I managed to arrange to have my father's friend, Sandy (the gentlemen who came to the hospital the night Jen was admitted), watch Rossella on the afternoons I had my support group. He lived in the neighboring town of Belmar and worked part time checking people as they entered the beach for their badges. I was relieved when he told me that he would watch Rossella so that I could go to my support group. The group had become a staple of stability for me. It was a constant in my life that I knew was good for me. Just as with many of the friends in the group, missing any of our weekly meetings just did not feel right. The group had become an essential meeting that helped us get through the grind and routines of daily life.

My father also pitched in. He came down to New Jersey and spent time with the girls and me during these few weeks and watched Rossella when I had my therapy appointments.

Additionally, there was even a night in which I had previously signed up to attend a charity comedy night that was sponsored by the center that ran my support group. It was a night that featured four comedians at a local theater, with all the proceeds going towards the center. I was determined to find someone to watch both girls that night. To my delight, Nicole's sister Kristen agreed to watch the girls, and I had a good time with some of my support group friends.

For the times I did have to venture out to Rossella's appointments or even to move her from place to place, she was able to elevate her leg in the wagon without hurting herself anymore. Plus, the wagon conveniently fit in the truck of my Honda Pilot. She received a lot of compliments from people, saying how cute it was that she was in her little red wagon.

The four weeks in which Rossella had her injured leg in a cast were actually in some ways a blessing for me. This time allowed me to be pushed to the limits, mentally, physically, and emotionally, so that I knew how much I was able to handle. I came out of this these grueling weeks in the summer of 2018, knowing that whatever obstacles and challenges came to me in the future, I would tackle them head on. Those weeks were difficult, demanding on many levels, and trying in ways that I can now appreciate only having been through all of it on my own. More so, my confidence as a single parent grew exponentially during this time. For four weeks flying solo, I was able to care for two children, one of whom could not walk on her own.

As I said earlier in the book, not only was this time like being dropped off at the base of Mount Everest without gear and told to climb to the summit of the mountain, but in addition you had to scale to the peak with a broken leg in a blinding snowstorm. Somehow, and in some way, I was able to get through all of this while still grieving the loss of Jen.

17

Jen's Corner

It was one of the nicest gestures I received after Jen's death. I was told by the girls' day care that I no longer had to pay their tuition. It was a huge burden off of my shoulders. I was highly appreciative, and I knew almost immediately I wanted to reciprocate the generosity to the day care.

When my finances were all in order, and winter was turning into spring, I knew it was time to propose my idea to Laurie, the director of the day care center. Placing something permanent at the day center in Jen's memory was a key part of my recovery.

When I made the initial request to the day care for a memorial for Jen, no one knew what the memorial should look like. All I told the day care was that it had to be something the day care needed, and that I was going to finance whatever it was. Both the girls' teacher, Ms. Cathy, and Laurie requested that they have a few weeks to make a decision, so that they could pick something that would not only benefit the center but also be a fitting commemorative. I agreed, and following a few weeks of anticipation, I was pleased to hear their decision because it would so perfectly represent Jen. The staff was allocating an unused, fenced in area of the day care grounds to build a playground Jen's memory. The playground would be constructed around two main themes: It would be extremely kid friendly and hands on for the children and all of the equipment and toys would be beach themed. I couldn't think of anything more quintessential Jen.

I was given the catalogs with some of the day care's suggestions earmarked with post-it notes. But I was given almost carte blanche on what could go into the 12' x 16' space. Even better, I was tasked with naming the playground. The name came to me almost instantly—Jen's Corner.

It took me only two days to comb through the catalogs and conduct an Internet search to decide on the equipment for Jen's Corner. Two big pieces of equipment would serve as the focal points: a 12' x 12' shaded structure with a fabric canopy cover and a high-density polyethylene plastic ship's bow. The canopy cover would be the blue of the ocean. The ship's bow would be great for climbing. Plus, the kids could pretend that they were on a real boat.

These custom-made items would take four weeks to arrive, and this would give me the time to put a team together to construct the equipment onsite when the parts were delivered to the school.

My good friend, Terri's husband, Adam, and two other fathers, Steve and Craig, volunteered to help with the installation. I was greatly moved by their generosity. These were all men who had actually never met Jen and did not really get to know me until after she died.

In addition to the canopy and ships bow, I had purchased some smaller toys for the playground area—a set of plastic fish with two fishing poles, a wavy tactile path that looked just likes waves in the ocean, a giant octoplay set that had interlocking pieces, and a sand and water activity play table. By the end of June, both the two large main items and all the small toys were delivered, and the other dads and I agreed we would work two July Sundays to install the equipment. Jen's brother agreed to participate on the Sunday we planned to install the ships bow. Everything was falling into place, and it looked like we were going to be able to get Jen's Corner installed and ready for August.

To my pleasure, one of the day care teacher's aides, who fell in love with the girls on her first day working at the school, agreed to babysit the girls on both Sundays so that neither childcare or Rossella's broken leg would prevent the project from moving forward. I was unstoppable in my overall plan to memorialize Jen. In the first place, she deserved this recognition. As important, creating something tangible of this magnitude to honor Jen would immensely help me with my recovery.

The extreme July heat may have interrupted construction, but when the playground was finally completed and the canopy and ships bow were in place, Jen's Corner looked exactly the way I had envisioned it four months prior when I ordered the equipment.

The first night the big equipment was in place, I

returned to the school with the girls and we stood and marveled at the ship and the canopy that represented the ocean. "This is Mommy's playground, I told them. "It will always be here as a reminder of how special your mommy was to everyone." As I took in the concreteness of the structure it occurred to me that finally something positive had come from this tragedy.

I waited until the following weekend to bring the smaller items to the playground. Laurie and the staff were thrilled when they saw the finished product. So were the kids who were at day care that day. The next task was to plan a dedication ceremony. I wanted it to be small and mandated that the girls' friends from school be the first kids to set foot on the playground.

August 1st, 2018, the day before Rossella's cast was scheduled to come off, was *the* date the event would take place. A sign saying "Jen's Corner" would be placed on the front gate of the playground and unveiled at the ceremony.

By August 1st, my anxiety was mounting, partly because I knew that I would have to speak at the ceremony. Even more, I was upset that I could no longer look forward to completing this project. That was another loss, smaller than my losses of the preceding months, but nonetheless a loss that would leave a hole in my life. Despite this, I felt nothing but peace and gratitude when we arrived at the day care center on that warm summer evening and saw all the parents and day care workers there with the girls and me. Even Dennis came down from Massachusetts to see how "Jen's Corner" had come to life.

Laurie opened the ceremony by instructing the parents, children, workers, and guests to hold hands around the playground. She spoke eloquently about Jen and recalled how much Jen loved Rossella and Giada and how much she enjoyed and cared for all the children at the school. When it was my turn to speak, I recited a reading that I had just received a few days earlier from my support group. It is called "My Silent Request":

Please talk about Jen even though she is gone.

I need to talk about her, and I need to do it over and over.

Be patient with my agitation. Nothing feels secure in my world.

Don't abandon me with the excuse that you don't want to upset me.

Get comfortable with my crying.

Sadness hits me in waves, and I never know when my tears may flow.

Just sit with me in silence, hold my hand.

Just because I look good does not mean that I feel good. Ask me how I feel only if you really have time to find out.

My grieving may only begin a few months after Jen's death. Don't think I will be over it in a couple of months or years. My whole world has crumbled, and I will never be the same.

Spread the word about what I need. So few know 'what to do' and I haven't the strength to teach everyone.

After reading that to everyone, it was time for the kids to enter the playground. Laurie wanted both Rossella and Giada to be the first children to walk on the sand and climb on the equipment. I did not prevent Rossella, who could now walk with the cast, from moving freely. and playing in the sand. The other ten children entered the playground, climbed on the ships bow, pretended to fish, and played with the sand/water table.

I stood and watched the kids jubilantly play in "Jen's Corner," and so many thoughts ran through my mind. Of course, I was still very much consumed with grief and sadness. Even though I knew—I felt—Jen's spirit was with me, I wanted her physically by my side. Some of the parents told me that Jen would have been proud of what I did. The word "would" was key. Speaking of Jen in the past tense was something new to me, and it was something I absolutely hated.

At the same time, I was overcome with strength and resolve. Following months of planning and coordination, everything had fallen into place. Seeing the playground complete and tangible before me transformed the negative feelings eating away at me into to something powerful and benevolent. I felt compelled to take action. The time had arrived for me to focus my energy on something positive, foster some type of altruistic and compassionate effort that would not only help people heal but also ensure that Jen's sprit never dimmed.

What would begin as an initial gesture of goodwill would transform into something that I would never before have imagined creating—the Jennifer Baldassarre Foundation.

18

JBF

Jen always viewed her education as something she earned by working hard, not something she was entitled to. She consistently pushed herself throughout high school and college to get high grades and honors. Just like me, she pushed through college to get her Bachelor's and Master's degrees in social work right out of high school without taking a break.

Jen took pride in these accomplishments throughout her life. She was the first person in her immediate family to attend and graduate from college. It was because of her degrees from Marywood University and the University of Pennsylvania that Jen was able to go onto work for the organization that she did.

Higher education was a cornerstone of her drive; it is what made Jen always pursue to achieve bigger and better things. I wanted to make sure that kids who had similar ambitions and who like Rossella and Giada had experienced a tremendous loss had an opportunity to pursue their dreams as well. Thus, in the spring of

2018, I laid out a plan for an annual Jennifer Baldassarre Memorial Scholarship at our local high school.

Simply put, the money put forth for that year was to be awarded to one graduating student who had been accepted to a college or university and who had lost a loved one (e.g., a parent, sibling, guardian, etc.). There would be no qualifying essay or other criteria necessary to apply. I did not believe it was in good taste to make students write an essay about their grief and loss in order to receive financial assistance for their higher education.

The student body was given approximately six weeks to apply for scholarships. In the meantime, I put aside the initial funding for the scholarship myself. As I began to tell people about the first scholarship award at the high school, the more people asked how they could contribute to the scholarship fund.

In the beginning, when I established the perpetual scholarship, I chose not to actively seek donations, but would have accepted and thanked anyone who wanted to contribute. As the weeks went by, however, more and more people wanted to participate. I decided that it was ridiculous to prevent people from contributing if they wanted to. Besides, this was all in Jen's memory, and based on the way people had helped the girls and me following Jen's passing, I knew a lot of people wanted to continue to help by supporting a good cause. For example, one of Jen's best work friends spearheaded a collection among her fellow employees and presented me with a check a couple of weeks prior to the award's presentation. And I set up a GoFundMe page and blasted the information about the donation site as many times as

I could on social media. Slowly, but steadily, donations came in for the scholarship fund.

By the end of April, the guidance counselor emailed me with the names of 15 applicants who had applied for the scholarship. Not all of the applicants had lost a parent or loved one. Only three students met that criteria. Of the three students who met the qualifications, there was one that immediately presented herself as the front runner for the award.

She was a senior who maintained straight A's throughout her four years of high school, had an impressive record of extracurricular activities and was going to The College of New Jersey to pursue a degree in secondary education. She managed to achieve all of these accomplishments even after losing both of her parents, and then her uncle who was her legal guardian within the span of just a couple of years. To further solidify my choice, she was a twin just like Rossella and Giada.

When I met with the guidance counselor to discuss the applications, the guidance counselor immediately said, "That's who I was hoping you were going to choose."

With that decision made, the next step was purchasing a plaque and incorporating Jen's picture. The plaque would be hung in the high school hallway. I was pleased that people would readily see the person that affected my life in so many positive ways. What's more, someday the girls would attend this school. How wonderful for Rosella and Giada to see how the scholarship founded in their mother's memory had helped so many students.

Finally, I began preparing a speech that I would

present when I awarded the scholarship. Just like Jen's eulogy, it had to be perfect. I was only going to get one chance to present the first scholarship, and I wanted Jen to be proud.

I had gone through several drafts of what I believed to be an appropriate and fitting speech. There were also moments when I had to stop writing because the emotions were too overwhelming—too raw—for me. In the end, though, I composed a speech that I timed at about three minutes long.

I showed the speech to a few people because I wanted feedback about my grammar, spelling, and word placement. Though there were not many revisions or corrections, my friend from the support group, who was an excellent proofreader, gave me some very useful suggestions and made the speech even better, more heartfelt and genuine. At that point, I knew the speech was perfect. I was ready for the presentation.

As Awards Night approached, friends and family expressed an interest in attending the ceremony. Josh and Nicole, our neighbors; Jen's friends from work, Donna, Pam, and Claudelle; Jen's Aunt Alletta and cousin Nada; and even Dennis, all planned on showing their support.

The girls and I arrived at the high school rather early on award's night. I purposely did this so that I could get settled in the seats without too much disruption for the girls. I had asked Donna to be with the girls while I was on stage. The school had arranged the order of presentations so that I would be speaking fourth, which was relatively early in the schedule.

The student government president stood at one

end of the stage and introduced each presenter. School administrators including the guidance counselor who assisted in the scholarship selection were seated center stage. When I was called to the stage, I took a deep breath, walked up to the stage and stood behind the podium, and said the following:

> **I stand here before everyone today as a man who lost his best friend and partner in life six months ago. My wife, Jen, was suddenly taken after suffering from cardiac arrest. She was at home, with our two daughters, Giada and Rossella, while helping to prepare Thanksgiving dinner for the next day.**
>
> **Many of you in this auditorium did not know my wife and when I chose to speak to all of you tonight, I was asked to share with everyone who she was. We only moved to Howell back in 2014, but I first met Jen in 1996 as freshman at Pocono Mountain High School in Pennsylvania. We graduated together in 2000. She went onto Marywood University and the University of Pennsylvania to pursue a career in social work. It was during this time that I witnessed Jen's desire to help those in need, and quite honestly, try to make the world a better place. She succeeded in doing so.**
>
> **Her strength, love, and determination to achieve greatness were just some of her many attributes. Jen was always there to help her friends, loved planning parties and events, and consistently**

pushed herself to become a better mother, wife, daughter, and sister. Jen's spirit, everything that made us love her, did not disappear six months ago. Her energy is here, alive with all of us, and will never diminish. It is something that can never be destroyed. It is something that will never fade. It will be here with each wave that crashes at the beach, through each setting sunset, through each passing holiday, and with each year that passes. In fact, it is her strength that is helping me on this stage tonight.

I witnessed Jen's kindness and generosity through the years, and this was what

ultimately made me fall in love with her. I once again experienced the same benevolence from many individuals when Jen fell ill and left us. The scholarship in Jen's memory is one of the ways in keeping her spirit alive, while paying forward a fraction of the goodwill and compassion that I was honored to have had in our time of need. This scholarship will be an annual award at Howell High School, providing assistance to one graduating senior who was accepted to a college or university and had experienced the loss of a loved one.

For its first year, the scholarship received numerous donations from individuals—some of whom I have never met that wanted to ensure that it got off on the right foot. I am proud to state that the first recipient of the scholarship is an individual who has worked hard throughout

her high school career and plans to attend the College of New Jersey for secondary education. She is someone who embodies the same values and beliefs as Jen. In addition, just like my two daughters, she is also a twin.

Ladies and gentlemen, it is my honor and privilege to present the 2018 Jennifer Baldassarre Memorial Scholarship to...

The award recipient came up on stage, I hugged her, handed her a check for $3,100, and she thanked me. I then proceeded down the stage steps to my seat, where I felt a huge weight lifted from my shoulders. When I arrived back at my seat, I noticed that a couple of my guests had cried; Dennis patted me on the back and told me, "Well done brother."

A few minutes went by and I noticed that my cell phone was continuously vibrating, receiving message from my friends and family who just saw my speech— Dennis and Nicole posted the video on Facebook, and people wanted to message me to tell me what they were moved by what they saw from me on stage. The feeling that I had the ability to affect so many people at once was something I experienced only one other time—when I gave the eulogy at Jen's funeral.

We left before the rest of the scholarships were presented. As we made our way to the lobby, I was approached by a teacher and a few other individuals who said they were greatly moved by my gesture and words.

My friends and family stayed in the lobby outside the

auditorium for a few minutes. They were still processing what it meant to present that first scholarship. We all reminisced about Jen for a little bit. Alletta and Nada both said that they were going to go to a diner for dinner and invited the girls and me. Everyone said their goodbyes at that point and left the school.

We made our way to a diner in Wall Township, about fifteen minutes from the school, and grabbed a corner booth. We wanted to catch up on how we were all doing, and to discuss how we all were processing the events of not only the last couple of hours, but the last couple of months.

While we were waiting for our food to come, my phone continued to blow up with text messages and the video of my speech on Facebook continued to receive likes and comments of support. My head was spinning, and thoughts about keeping the scholarship going and what to do to pick up momentum for this cause raced through my mind. Five weeks later, the Jennifer Baldassarre Foundation, or JBF as it is more commonly called, was formed as an official 501(c)(3) non-profit organization.

Of course, one of the first things I had to do was hire an attorney, one who specialized in the formation of non-profit organizations. The next step: a tax attorney. My accountant referred me to a tax attorney in Red Bank, New Jersey.

Within a week I was in Red Bank speaking with the tax attorney about the intentions of JBF and why it was important to me to get all of the federal and state paperwork done as soon as possible. As part of the initial filing, I had to pick members for a Board of Directors. This came to me rather easily: Dennis, Josh, Nicole, and Nada were the first names that came to my mind. There were two additional people that I wanted on the JBF board: my friend Barbara with whom Jen and I had worked at different times, and my friend Nicole D. with whom I worked years ago.

In what seemed like no time, the Board of Directors was in place, and the attorney began filing the necessary paperwork and completing the many steps necessary for JBF's formation: applying for a federal Employer Identification Number, filing an official article of incorporation, drafting by-laws, and getting a state tax ID number. The last document required involved the approval of the foundation's tax-exempt status, which allowed people to make charitable, tax-deductible donations. Within 45 days, I had in hand all the required paperwork to make JBF a legitimate charity in the state of New Jersey.

There was one other item was a post office box that would allow mail to get delivered to a location that was not my home address, which was a requirement for all charitable organizations. To me, there was only one place that was fitting to have JBF's PO Box and that was Avon-by-the-Sea. I went down to the post office and reserved the post office box. Not too long after, I received a very definite sign from Jen. One afternoon I pulled into our local Wawa and noticed a car with Pennsylvania license plates that read *JBF-0391*. An almost exact number, 391"is the PO Box number for JBF. I would continuously get signs from Jen, or so I believe, from license plates, specifically those that read *JBF* or *JEN*.

Several people and one corporation donated money to JBF. A donation came from one of Jen's friends who donated money in lieu of giving out favors at her upcoming wedding. Another donation came from my friend and former co-worker who lives in Massachusetts. He had given me a sizable donation when I was up in Massachusetts for a client's open house. Momentum was building for JBF, and I needed to keep it going. I decided that the time had come to call the first board meeting to determine the foundation's direction.

I had my cousin, Anthony, from New York, build a JBF website. All non-profits and charitable organizations require a web and social media presence to promote awareness for their causes and have a platform through which they can ask for and receive donations. In addition, it was another way to tell people who Jen was and how much she meant to the twins and me as well as a lot of other people.

Anthony sent me website templates that were made especially for non-profits. One of the first templates I saw on his list caught my attention. A significant portion of the main page was included a revolving series of pictures. The idea hit me: my pictures of Avon-by-the-Sea would be placed on this website with the logo of JBF imposed in the pictures.

There was also an additional space on the main page that allowed for narratives, and this was going to be the space that would permit me to write specific narratives about Jen and JBF's mission. When it came time to draft JBF's mission statement, I had no trouble writing it:

To establish and maintain a successful tribute to Jennifer by financially assisting the needs of students who wish to advance their education and who have also experienced the loss of a parent or loved one.

In addition to the mission statement, I superimposed a phrase from my presentation speech about *Jen's energy never diminishing or being destroyed* on a picture of ocean waves on the website. That part of the speech, had, and still has, significant meaning to me. The belief that somehow there is a part of Jen, albeit not visible to the eye but present in my heart, that survived and did not disappear entirely provided great comfort to me in the months following Jen's death. Dennis and others repeatedly told me that energy cannot be created or destroyed, and, hence, Jen is never really gone. She is watching over the girls and me.

Over the course of several weeks and with Anthony's help, the website gradually came together. It was actually pretty incredible to witness something that was conceived through rough ideas turn into something that the entire world could see. I knew that JBF was picking up even more momentum. There was yet another way for me to get the word out—Foundation car magnets and the #jbfacrossamerica campaign.

19

#JBFAcrossAmerica

The original idea for JBF car magnets started out as a concept one day in the spring of 2018. Every worthwhile cause has a noteworthy media campaign that's quick and easy to get underway at little or no cost. For several weeks, I contemplated the best approach for my campaign.

Finally, one day it hit me—magnets. They are a lot easier to keep on a car and a lot of people were more inclined to have a magnet on their car than a bumper sticker. Magnets are, very popular. Lots of people have them on their cars for a variety of reasons. In addition, JBF car magnets were a surefire way to advertise the organization.

I had to shop around among various online vendors, because not all of the sites I reviewed sold magnets in the size I wanted. More importantly, only some of the vendors would use the logo colors on the magnet. The logo had two distinct types of shading: a bright orange that gradually faded into a bright green. There were also waves, just like at the beach, that formed the shape of the bottom of the logo. It was not completely circular. The bottom had a more linear shape so that the entire logo looked remarkably like a horse shoe crab.

I finally found a website that allowed me to recreate the logo's shape and colors, and I initially ordered a couple dozen magnets. It only took about five days to get the order, and when they came in, my car was the first one to have a magnet placed on it. I posted a picture on the Facebook and Instagram pages that I had created for the Foundation. Within a day or two, I had given magnets to Dennis and Barbara, as well as to my father, and, very quickly, JBF was represented in New Jersey, Pennsylvania, and Massachusetts.

Then I received a message on Facebook from a high school friend wanting a magnet, so I mailed it the next day. I requested that they send me a picture of the magnet on their car so that I could post it on social media.

Following the posting of that picture, I received requests from family and friends in New York, New Hampshire, Virginia, and Illinois for JBF magnets, as well as from more people in New Jersey. I did not want money for the magnets. All I asked was for people to send me a picture of the magnets on their cars, refrigerators, or wherever they decided to stick the magnet so that I could post the picture on all the JBF social media channels.

I started receiving multiple pictures a day. I found a website that allowed you to color in each state on a map of the United State using different colors. So, I started to use the website, and each time I received a picture from a new state I would fill that state in and post the updated map on social media. Nicole, who by this time was the secretary for the JBF Board of Directors, suggested that the magnet campaign needed a hashtag so that people could tag it and make JBF an even bigger movement. That's how the hashtag #jbfacrossamerica was born.

Throughout the months of August and September 2018, the number of cities and states grew rapidly. Coppell, Texas; Windsor, Connecticut; Allentown, Pennsylvania; New York City; Westchester, Ohio; and Raleigh, North Carolina all had magnets within the first few weeks. By the end of August, JBF had magnets in seventeen states, mostly on the east coast of the United States. Then, JBF made its way to the west coast and Eugene, Oregon, almost 3,000 miles away, thanks to the help of a friend from Berwick, Maine.

Some of our friends and family caught onto the hashtag campaign and wanted to help me get as many magnets out, so that JBF would have magnets in all fifty states. I sent them magnets and they sent them to their friends in various parts of the country. By the middle of October, with their help, I got magnets out to places in which I did not know anyone: Springdale, Arkansas; Peoria, Arizona; Birmingham, Alabama; Woodstock, Georgia; and even Boulder Creek, California. Groups were also interested in having the magnets. Jen's former co-workers fell into this category as did neighbors, the people who were there for me the in the days following Jen's death. By the end of October, five houses on my block had JBF magnets on all of their cars. On some days, when I would be driving home, I would see magnets leading up to my house.

In fact, JBF magnets were being showcased all over New Jersey and across the country. It made me feel that Jen's spirit was not only present to me but also to others far and wide. It was gratifying to view the magnets in so many different places and among people who did not even know Jen. I felt as though a little piece of her spirit was watching over all these people.

It was also rewarding for me to know that one of my goals for 2018 was turning into a reality. I was giving people hope and comfort, changing a tragedy of unimaginable proportions into a force of benevolence and charity for so many different people.

One day after what would have been our 11-year wedding anniversary, October 21st, 2018, I returned to the medium I went to earlier that year. I desperately wanted to talk to Jen—to have some kind of dialogue with her. (Widows and widowers will try absolutely anything to establish some form of communication with their departed spouses). Right at the start of our session, the medium told me that Jen was proud of the fundraising that I was doing. Oddly enough, one of the primary reasons I had visited the medium was so Jen could tell me if she approved of JBF and the scholarship award. And here Jen was, telling the medium she believed in everything I was doing with the charity work.

JBF was now fully established. It had a board, a mission statement and a reputation. This imbued me with something that I had lacked for some time—a new perspective on life. I felt incredibly fortunate. I was tremendously grateful. I was working hard to spread the word about Jen and her compassion and goodwill. I was redirecting my energy into something palpable. This made me realize that material things are not as important as helping others. The actions and decisions that we all make in life are what really matter. Treating others the way we want to be treated, especially in times of tragedy and disaster, defines who we are as a people. JBF is not only part of Jen, it is also a part of me. What's more, it is surely a piece of all the lives the foundation touches—board members, award recipients, and JBF supporters.

Perhaps American essayist Ralph Waldo Emerson says this best for me:

The purpose of life is not to be happy. It is to be useful, to be honorable, to be compassionate, to have it make some difference that you have lived and lived well.

Jen was all these things in life, and she definitely made a difference. JBF will continue to live up to these ideals in her honor. It will also continue to guide me for the rest of my life.

20

Survivor's Guilt

There are many consequences that come when dealing with the sudden loss of a spouse, both expected and unexpected. There are some that I would consider manageable and others that completely overwhelmed me to the point where I was not able to function.

In the months following Jen's death, I suffered vivid and, in some cases, gruesome nightmares. The events in those nightmares were violent. I am not ashamed or uncomfortable to admit that I feared having those dreams and, as a result, required a prescription for Ambien, a sleep aid that pretty much guaranteed me some amount of sleep, albeit restless sleep.

The daytime panic attacks were to some extent horrific and just as crippling as the nightmares. Playing out the scene in which Jen collapsed, and waiting for the ambulance would become a regular occurrence and I'd have to deal with these attacks in order to get through the day. Thankfully, with the help of therapy, medication, and the support of many people who assisted me during my darkest times, I managed to get the attacks under control, avoid a total shut-down and be an attentive father to the girls.

There was one part of my journey, however, that caught me off guard and became a significant obstacle in my recovery: the burdensome survivor's guilt.

The pain I endured on an almost regular basis was tremendous and something I would never have predicted. I would have to convince myself that it was not my fault that Jen died, that I could not have prevented this, no matter what I would have done differently. Here I was, still alive, caring for our two kids, and trying to tell myself that it was all right to grant myself permission to still enjoy life, as much as I possibility could when at times all I wanted to do was break down and cry.

This is still part of my struggle. Jen loved life, she loved her daughters, loved the life that we had built for each other, and she was no longer here to enjoy it. How was this possible? How was I able to still live a happy life without the person who made me the happiest? To further complicate things, I would later discover that my survivor's guilt was somehow acting as a protective factor for me. My guilt was keeping my bond with Jen intact somehow, and I believed that if I lost that connection with Jen, I would no longer have any way to keep her close to me. Subconsciously I did not want to give that up. So, in an extremely odd way, I was my own worst enemy.

There were several things I did to allow myself to heal, recover, and continue to live life. First, as odd or as simple as this may sound, I repeatedly told myself that Jen was gone—that I was never going to see her in this life again, and that I still had to live. I had to keep telling myself this over and over again, in some cases, multiple times a day. It did not take away any of the pain; it just forced me to be realistic so that I could focus on another important point: understanding that Jen would have wanted me to live and enjoy life, because I would have wanted the same thing for her.

In the early months of 2018, several people told me that I had to continue on—that I needed to live life again, but, at that time, those were just words; they did not resonate with me. As a matter of fact, when people said that to me, it just irritated me, and quite frankly, angered me.

Then, as time went on, my thought process began to change, and I had an epiphany. I would have to push myself to live again and to enjoy what life did have to offer. Whether it was something as simple as smelling the sea air in Avon-by-the-Sea or things that needed more focus and attention like JBF, I had come to tell myself that Jen would not have wanted me to live the rest of my life surrounded by grief. I was almost able to hear Jen whispering in my ear: "Joseph, I cannot rest in peace unless you are living. We will see each other soon enough, but you need to take care of yourself and our girls."

There was one final principle that helped me overcome my survivor's guilt: learning to detach myself from feelings and thoughts that had a negative effect on my well-being. At first, this was impossible, and then transformed into a behavior I practiced daily. The practice of separating myself from thoughts that are constantly bringing me down is not easy. It takes time, patience, and most importantly energy, but little by little, is something that can be accomplished. Once I began to realize that it could be done, it became a valuable tool in my toolbox on the road to recovery.

There are still times where I will feel guilty that I am still alive, and my partner in life is physically no longer with me. Like on any road, there will be dips, sharp turns, and an occasional pot hole. Still, I learned that I am behind the wheel, driving the car as best as I can, focused on my destination. Even though my co-pilot may be gone, I am not alone on my journey, and I am going to try and enjoy the ride as much as I can.

21

Reevaluating Priorities

There are many parts of my last day with Jen, November 22nd, 2017, that will forever be engrained in my mind. I remember the project I was working on for my employer that morning and how I was complaining to Jen how no one at my job seemed to truly appreciate what I was doing for them.

I remember I was concerned that Jen and I would be able to fit in a movie, because we had numerous errands to run throughout the day as well as prepare for Thanksgiving the following day. This included Jen making a trip that morning to a local orchard in order to pick up a holiday pie and vegetables, the green beans she was cooking at the exact moment when her heart stopped, and she fell to the floor.

Also, I vividly remember that during the day I was burning a couple of pine-scented candles throughout the house to put us in a festive mood. Then, the whole time we were at the movies, I worried whether I had extinguished the candles before we left the house. I was actually afraid that something bad was going to happen that day!

Then, in a matter of a few moments that evening, my entire world was forever changed. I had gone from worrying about whether Jen and I were going to have enough time to get all of our errands done to watching my wife being taken out of our house and put into an ambulance. I had gone from concern about blowing out the candles when we left the house to making sure our daughters did not watch their mother take her last breath. And then ultimately, I witnessed Jen leaving this world.

It took a while for me to see the exact lesson in all of this, but I eventually did when the shock wore off, and I was able to process my thoughts in an appropriate way. I learned that my priorities were grossly out of whack. This disaster showed me that there are more important things in this world then making sure that I got my way at work or ensuring that all my errands were done.

There are things in life that are truly priceless: like being with the ones you love; holding their hand during a movie; talking about what will excite them during the upcoming holidays; or simply saying I love you and starring at them and trying to make a memory. All of these things are absolutely the top priorities in life. These are the moments that will not only get you through a hard day but will also get you through the difficult times. They'll provide comfort you when you need it most and will outlast the test of time and struggle. Jen had understood this and tried to surround the girls and me with these moments whenever she could. I am so thankful that she did, because I have needed those moments to fill my thoughts after she left.

It took me months to fully accept the notion that the way in which I had lived life in the past, worrying about issues that should not be a priority, was not the way to live now. It never was. Does it really matter if my co-workers upset me? No, it does not because at the end of the day, it is just a job. Does it really matter if all my errands are not done in the way I want them to be? No, it does not because the errands will get done at some point. Does it really matter if your plans do not pan out the way that you thought they would? Of course not. There are lots of things that do not go the way they are supposed to.

What really matters is that you tell the people who mean the most to you in life how much they have an impact on your life and how special they are—and, most importantly, how much you love them, even when times are bad or disaster strikes.

One of the five stages of grief is bargaining, and this stage was, and in some cases is, still the hardest for me. My mind was flooded with questions like "What if I did this?" and "What if I had realized that earlier?" It took considerable mental energy and time to realize these types of questions drain my mental stamina. Instead, if you live life telling the people you love how special they are to you—if you make the most of what you are given, then if something bad happens, you are not holding yourself hostage to feelings of doubt and distrust.

Most importantly, does anyone actually remember the small things that cause the daily stressors? I had plenty of fights and disagreements with Jen, and many disappointments. Now, looking back on everything, I cannot remember how a single fight started, or what was said during those arguments, or even how we resolved those quarrels. None of that matters to me now.

What I do remember, and what I do care most about are the wonderful moments we had together—shared moments of happiness and joy.

I have so many bad memories of November 22nd, 2017, but the one thing I will forever remember about that day—truly one of the best moments in my life— was holding Jen's hand while we were at the movie. As simple as it was, it is a memory I will always cherish. It will be etched in my mind forever and I will draw from it whenever I need strength in my life.

22

An Island of Emotional Comfort

I have gone to visit Jen at her resting place during all different times of the day. I have gone mostly in the mornings, and sometimes in the afternoons. I have even gone a couple of times after it has gotten dark. At night, there is a light that is directly above her crypt so that I am able to see her picture and so that I do not trip over any of the shrubbery or landscaping that surrounds the mausoleum. I have travelled to the cemetery during the brightest and sunniest of days, gone during torrential downpours, freezing cold winter days, and everything in between. I even attempted to go there right after a huge snowstorm when the cemetery grounds were not shoveled and plowed out. I felt as though it was my obligation to be there with Jen as much as I possible regardless of what Mother Nature threw my way.

There was one time and one day in particular when I really enjoyed visiting Jen—very early on Monday mornings, right before 9 a.m. There are two reasons for this: first, everyone is busy starting their week, rushing to work, or rushing to get their kids off to school. As the world around me is moving at this fast pace, I can have my time and space with Jen and this provides an island of emotional comfort, as I have come to call it. In my head, the world continues to speed by. But for a little bit of time, maybe only ten minutes, the world around me is at my pace. This slower motion allows all the ordinary things others are doing to pass me by and gives me the quiet time to grieve, reflect, express my love, or do whatever I have to do on any given day.

The second reason is that Monday mornings are the quietest time at the cemetery. The quiet enables me to relax and replay my memories of my time with Jen. On the weekends, there are always a lot of visitors, and they interrupt my moments with Jen.

As 2018 progressed, the thought that I would be travelling to my island for emotional comfort for years became more of a reality. Even the very idea of Jen's final resting place being my island was true in a geographical sense. To the east is New Jersey Route 18, a busy highway in Monmouth and Middlesex counties, and to the west is the Garden State Parkway. Interstate 195 is to the south, and Route 33 is to the north of the cemetery, hence the feeling of being on an island. This image gives me solace, because I know I can escape there—always.

Right from the start of these trips to the cemetery, I would imagine that Jen was leaving this sacred island with me. And I could feel her presence, sitting in the car next to me, holding my hand, and comforting me for the rest of my day.

For young widows/widowers, trips to a spouse's cemetery or a final resting place like the World Trade Center site in New York City become commonplace and afford an ongoing bond with a loved one. Jen's resting place will be a place of peace for me for decades. No matter where, a widow or widower must create *own* island of comfort—a place that is so special that absolutely no one can understand its significance, nor should they try.

Although I will always take my daughters to their mother's final resting place, not even they will totally understand why I created this spiritual safe zone. This island—my island –will sustain me, be burnished in my heart, soul and mind, and I will tend it for years to come. That's a certainty and my good fortune, because it will allow me a never-ending connection with Jen.

23

The Ultimate
Litmus Test

As cliched as it sounds, a widower's life will dramatically change, and it will do so whether he wants it to or not. There is no denying it. A widower's life will transform into something that is almost unrecognizable when compared with the life he lived prior to his spouse's death.

There will come a time, however, in which the pain and suffering caused by the passing of his partner will become a part of him. It will no longer overwhelm his being. It will simply become a part of who he is.

The event that turned things around for me was my visit to the psychic medium in October 2018. That was when something inside of me clicked and said: "Jen is gone, there is nothing I could have done to stop it, and Jen would have wanted me to live my life." After leaving the medium that day, a thought hit me like a thunderbolt: I had lost a year of my life, and I was never getting it back.

Thus, following these realizations, I knew that I had to establish a rudimentary system for keeping things in check for me mentally and emotionally. I called this check and balance system the ultimate litmus test.

The test is really a simple way of keeping a tight rein on my grief so that I can start living again. The test consists of two steps: 1) asking myself if Jen had the ability to communicate with me, would she be happy with how I was raising the girls and happy that I was happy and 2) when it comes to telling friends and family about anything, would they be happy for me? If the answer from others would be no, then the odds are that those individual(s) would not support me during my continued recovery. I would have to tune them out.

This is how I applied the litmus test in 2018 and how it worked:

In the fall, my friends Josh and Nicole were the first ones to invite my daughters and me to spend Thanksgiving Day with them. Being that the anniversary of Jen's death fell on Thanksgiving Day, I knew I had to be at the cemetery that morning. Then I wanted an extremely low-key holiday, with the opportunity to drink wine as possible (of course, not becoming too inebriated to care for the girls). I knew Jen would have been happy with my plan, because it made the girls and me happy. For the most part, almost everyone agreed with my decision, and I felt the backing of my support network of close-knit friends and family.

Young widows and widowers like me have enough challenges to overcome and enough battles to fight. If there is one thing that helps them in their recovery, it is support. I have simply learned that if you are not part a solution, then you are part of the problem. As my friend Dennis has repeatedly told me: "Stay solution focused."

The bottom line is that widows and widowers need to do what they feel is right, what makes them feel better, not just for themselves, but for anyone who must rely on them for support. Perhaps the Ultimate Litmus Test can be another tool in the toolbox for widows and widowers. I know it will be in mine. It is a tool I did not have before, nor did I need it. Now that I do have it, it will make me wiser and more insightful and serve as an indispensable resource as I embark upon a new life passage.

24

365 Days and Nights

As Halloween passed, and the calendar turned to November, I began to mentally prepare myself for the one-year anniversary of Jen's passing. (As I explained before, I did not count December 11th as Jen's death. She clinically died at our house on November 22nd).

My support group friends shared how they had coped with and viewed their one-year anniversaries. Everyone in the group kept saying, "Have a plan." Yes, it is important to have a plan, but I knew that I had to keep the day simple, and not overextend myself in any way. I did not want to find myself in a position in which I was overwhelmed with emotions that were barreling at me like waves against a pier during a hurricane. I knew that a storm was coming, and I had to prepare so that I would be able to ride it out—no matter what was thrown my way. At one point, I did find myself taking note that never in my wildest dreams would I have thought that I would have to mentally prepare myself for a death anniversary. But here I was, indeed formulating a game plan.

Since the anniversary was on Thanksgiving Day, I already knew that the girls and I would pay our respects to Jen that morning and just "take it all in." We would place flowers at her grave and enjoy the peacefulness of the moment. Then I knew that I would be we would go to Josh and Nicole's that afternoon for dinner. As it turned out, it all fell in place rather easily, and that was a blessing.

The Friday before Thanksgiving I did keep to our tradition, and I put up the Christmas tree for the girls. Knowing my limits, I had made the decision months before that I was not going to put up all the Christmas decorations. Still, the Christmas tree being in place and decorated before Thanksgiving was something, I wanted to do for all of us.

Putting the artificial tree up was a relatively easy task, but the harder part was getting the lights up on the tree. Jen had always placed the strings of LED lights on the tree, and it took her hours. I was usually outside stringing the lights up on bushes and front stair railings, but this year I chose to go with more subdued decorations, which was absolutely acceptable. Also, I did not want to take down and pack away a lot of decorations, like I did the year prior when it took me two days to take everything down by myself.

My goal was to get the tree up and lit before I had to pick up the girls from school that afternoon. I worked non-stop and was successful in meeting my objective.

Getting the Christmas tree back up in 2018 was a significant milestone in my recovery. After Jen had collapsed, I was, in a manner of speaking, forced to look at all the Christmas decorations in my home while Jen laid in a hospital bed on a respirator. Having the tree back up did a couple of things for me. It meant that the one-year anniversary was coming quickly and potentially I could have flashbacks of the pain we had suffered the year before. It did, however, symbolize that indeed it had been a year. I had survived a year without Jen and endured the misery that filled those 365 days and nights. It was a tangible reminder that I actually had made it— that life could continue after a tragic event like that.

Friday evening, the girls and I finished decorating the tree with all the ornaments that Jen and I had accumulated during the 11 years of our marriage. Some ornaments had been handed down from my parents. At the end of the night, the girls were excited that their Christmas tree was back up in the living room, and kept staring at it in awe, asking me where some of the ornaments had come from.

For the next few nights, I stayed out in the living room longer than usual after Giada and Rossella had gone to bed so that I could enjoy the fruits of our labor. While not all of the decorations were out, there were enough to ensure that the girls would experience the excitement of the holiday season.

For the week of Thanksgiving, parent-teacher conferences meant that Giada and Rossella had shortened days at school. Dismissal time was 12:45 p.m. in lieu of their normal time of 2:30 p.m. I used the time while they were at school to get some consulting work done for my clients. I also allowed myself to mentally recharge my batteries so that when the girls came home, I would be able to put my best foot forward for them, and not allow myself to get depressed or upset because of the anniversary.

The day before Thanksgiving, November 21ˢᵗ, 2018, started off like any other of the previous days that month. I awoke at 6:30 a.m. and got the girls dressed and prepared for school. I dropped them off at 8:00 a.m. and then went straight home to continue my work.

I was drafting a new set of standard operating procedures for my client in my home office, and as I was doing this, I had Christmas music playing over my Amazon Dot. Then, as quick as flipping a switch, it suddenly hit me: I was in the exact location, completing the same tasks on which I was working at the same time one year earlier.

I literally stopped mid-sentence with what I was writing, got up and left my office. I began to have the flashbacks about the exact activities of the previous year— from the work I was doing that morning, to when Jen and I went to the movies, to the events that occurred that evening at the house and hospital. I was drowning in my memories, and I needed to quickly pull myself out of it. I knew I had to leave the house. So, I went down to Home Depot and purchased real pine wreaths for the front of my house. I needed the distraction, and I assumed that this was the best thing I was able to do at the time.

Even when I got home, I did not want to go back in the house. I stayed outside, in my car until it was time to pick up my daughters at school. I simply did not want to be alone in the house surrounded by the memories of what had happened one year ago.

The girls' appointment with their therapist that evening was the saving grace that kept me out of the house. Additionally, I was treating the girls to McDonalds, which meant we would be out longer.

The girls had a productive session with their therapist, and just as usual, a trip to McDonalds followed. As I sat and ate, I watched the girls playing on the indoor playground, having fun with the other kids, and began to reflect on what had occurred earlier. Was this how it was going to be on every milestone? Were the girls really going to be fine growing up without their mother? These were only some of the questions that played out in my mind, but then I had an epiphany: I was at the height of the storm and experiencing the biggest rush of my emotions. If I was able to get through this, then, metaphorically, there was going to be a finish line.

The sun had set by the time we left McDonalds, and the darkness and chill of the November air had brought me back to the night that Jen was admitted to the hospital. I remembered that night. I was locked outside the hospital and had to walk around to the other entrance in the freezing cold without a jacket. But tonight, this night, I just had to hang in there for a few more hours until I reached the finish line—until I was able to state that I had made it one full year in my grief, one year without Jen.

I had planned to put some type of message on social media for everyone to read in tribute of Jen, as well as to inform everyone that I was doing all right that night at midnight. I had written something on my cell phone earlier that day when I escaped from my house. I had put the finishing touches on it while I was in the waiting room during the girls' therapy appointment. However, I was receiving text messages from a variety of different people throughout the day. It did not seem right having people wait until midnight to hear what I had to say, so I placed the following statement on my Facebook and Instagram accounts:

> Tomorrow will be 365 days since the worst day of my life and the girls' lives. The world would have spun around on its axis 365 times. The sun would have risen in the east and set in the west 365 times. I would have awakened 365 times without the woman I loved next to me, since I have been 17, and have fallen asleep 365 times absent of her physical presence.

> In the last 365 days, I had to say my final goodbyes, plan a funeral lost my job due to "budgetary cuts," had to help Rossella heal after she broke her leg and could not walk for 5 weeks, and watched my daughters start kindergarten without their mother.

> However, in the midst of all of the tragedy, pain, and sadness, life has gone on. Albeit not been the same, and truly unrecognizable, we are all still here, missing Jen everyday. One of the things that has gotten me through the past 12 months is trying to hold onto something positive, even if that positive 'something' had to be created. The initial memorial scholarship award in Howell back in June, JBF was formed and will continue

to make its presence felt, helping students who also experienced a similar pain and loss. A new playground stands at the girls' old daycare center in Brick, which will be used by hundreds of kids in the years to come. Most importantly, Giada and Rossella continue to be Jen's ultimate legacy. They are healthy, happy, and continue to ask about their mother.

To everyone who has helped me and my family for the past 365 days, thank you. We were all on this journey together, one that no one should ever travel. And remember, even though Jen is not here, she is WITH all of us.

Within hours of posting that message on social media, my phone blew up with text messages from my friends and family just like it did after my speech at Howell High School back in June. And it would continue. Throughout the night and into the next day people posted comments on my pages,

November 22nd, Thanksgiving Day, finally arrived. It was the day that I had been anticipating for some time. This year the day was unusually frigid and windy; it was the coldest Thanksgiving Day I could remember in a long time.

I had gotten the girls dressed and ready to brave the cold to visit their mother's crypt Knowing that the stores were going to either be closed or mobbed on Thanksgiving morning, I had purchased flowers the day before, to bring to Jen's grave Thanksgiving morning.

Arriving at the cemetery that morning, the atmosphere was very quiet—no else was there. I had each of the girls bring a flower to her grave. I just hugged them both and took a deep breath.

We stayed at the cemetery for quite some time. For once, we were not actually crying. We headed home to get ready to go to Josh and Nicole's, and I was very much looking forward to spending the day with my friends and having a distraction. Throughout the afternoon, the text messages kept rolling in from people sending me their thoughts and prayers for the girls.

We went over to Josh and Nicole's around 1:00 p.m., and the girls dove right into playing dress-up and building pillow forts with their friend, Lily. Nicole and Josh had set me up with a festive alcoholic beverage, and I finally got to relax.

A couple of days before Thanksgiving, I had purchased some caviar from the local farm stand (the same one that Jen had gone to one year prior for Thanksgiving and brought it with me to their house as an appetizer. I never had caviar before, and I wanted to try something new with my friends. It was also a small way of celebrating that I had made it a year without Jen, and I wanted to share that joy. We stayed at Josh and Nicole's for dinner and dessert, had a few laughs and enjoyed each other's company.

It was around 6:00 p.m. when the girls and I made our way back home. I had turned on the Christmas tree lights and the other lights in the house before we left so that when it got dark, the house would already be illuminated for our 30 second walk home. The girls were exhausted from playing with Lily, so much so that they fell asleep early on the couch. I helped them to bed and then I stayed up for a while longer, enjoyed the lights, and took it all in. I had survived a year, one year since the worst day of my life. The next day was the start of a new chapter.

25

Isolation Paradox

In the twelve months that followed Jen's passing, there were certainly plenty of times that I found myself surrounded by family and friends. This was especially true early in 2018 when many people routinely called me or texted me, or even wanted to take me out to lunch or dinner. These were times when it would seem I most needed the company, but when I actually found myself wanting to be alone. I did not have any desire to take part in conversations. I especially did not want to look at other happily married couples, realizing what I no longer had with Jen.

Then there were other times in the course of the year I found myself not conversing with anyone, finding myself not being invited to certain activities, and wanting to be included in whatever people were doing. I would go onto my social media pages, and I would consistently see my family and friends doing something fun and exciting. I would be upset that I was not invited, questioning whether or not I inadvertently did something that made people not want to invite or even see me. There were times when I wondered if people could not even be with me, because they were still upset about what had happened to Jen, and it would get them more distraught.

All these thoughts plagued me for some time. I came to refer to these conflicting thoughts as the isolation paradox. I either found myself either wishing to be left alone when lots of people wanted to be around me to provide comfort and their friendship. Or, I found myself alone, with the sense that I was being completely shut out when I needed to have people surround me and include me in activities. This absolutely did not help me in my recovery, and I always seemed to be complaining about this to anyone who would listen to me.

It was easy to get sucked into the isolation paradox. One day, right around the one-year anniversary mark, I said "Enough." I realized that this type of internal conflict was not going to get me anywhere. I was just going to be spinning my tires in the mud.

I decided then that the isolation paradox was no longer going to have any type of hold on me—that it was not going to influence the way I lived my life. If I wanted people to be in my life, then I had to make an effort to make sure they were. I had to take initiative so that my relationships were reciprocal. I had people who cared about me and I would care about them -- always, not just when it was convenient for me.

I also concluded that I needed to start breaking down the artificial mental barriers that I created to protect myself, because I needed to start living life again. I had in some ways stopped enjoying life because survivor's guilt prevented me from doing so. The amount of time and energy it would ultimately take for me to chisel away at these obstacles and mental roadblocks would be significant. It would be one of my greatest challenges, because I had indeed lost a year of my life, and in that period, I had gotten a little rusty. I wanted to lose neither more time nor more of myself. Now, there was a need for action. It was time to rejoin the world.

26

Losing a Whole Year

Like the Third Eye Blind song, my relationship with Jen did come to an end, but it was not because of a breakup, but rather something that neither of us planned nor controlled.

There was no dispute. I had lost a year of my life, and when that realization hit, it struck me in such a way that I was taken aback. It greatly depressed me. I was 35 years old, and a widower with two kids. No one would have ever thought that would happen, least of all, me. Jen was gone, and there was nothing that I could do to bring her back; no way to actually communicate with her, and I was on my own. In a way, widows and widowers are abandoned, and they are left to pick up the pieces.

There was one day in the fall of 2018, a couple of weeks before *the* anniversary where it literally shook me that I had lost so much—my job, my personal security, my mental health, and even some of my memory skills. Just like pregnant woman who legitimately have baby brain, there is a similar concept called widow's brain, which caused me to have difficulty remembering names, phone numbers, and even some memories. In time, all of these things could come back to me. But it would take hard work on my part and require me to change the way I looked at the world.

There were, however, two things that were irreplaceable and could not be given back to me, no matter how hard I wished, tried, or geared up emotionally and physically. The first was obviously Jen: no one will ever replace Jen, nor do I ever want anyone to. My life with her can never be replicated, and I would never compare any future partner that I may have to her.

The second thing that was irreplaceable was the year of my life that began when Jen fell ill and passed away to the first anniversary of her death in 2018. It is not as if I had a time machine from H.G. Wells that permitted me to go back twelve months and prevent the events that transpired. This length of time had passed and there was no way to get any of it back. When I realized this, I told my father that I might as well be 36 years old, not 35. The whole time I was 35 did not feel like I lived for that year, so I might as well just skip ahead in age by a year. That one year of living was purely about survival, plain and simple.

In time, I did the only thing that I was able to do with this epiphany—accept it, move on, and put it behind me. Why should I dwell on trying to fix something that could not be fixed? If I used my mental stamina trying to correct something that could not be corrected, what was the point?

Additionally, I also knew that if Jen was able

to communicate directly with me, she would tell me straight out that she would want me to live my life and be happy, so that I could take care of our daughters. I now use that as a motivator for feeling better and for coping and trying to move forward. It is part of my new perspective. In the course of a year, I had acquired one important addition to my toolbox: looking at the world through the unique lens that I acquired as a widower.

27

Rose Colored Glasses

Simply put, I do wear rose-colored glasses, in a symbolic sense. These glasses are worn by widows and widowers all the time, but they cannot be seen by others. I am the only one who can see my glasses, and they are probably the greatest tool in my toolbox.

For twelve months, from November 2017 to November 2018, I have been broken down, and in some ways, rebuilt from the ground up. The old Joe is no longer here. In a way, the old me passed away with Jen. What I mean by this is that the beliefs I had and the way I lived my life with Jen are gone, and I will never go back to being like that again.

I now have many new philosophies about how to live life. Obviously, the first is that I can no longer take anything for granted. Life is too short, and it can be over without any warning. Every time I breathe, walk, talk, and hold my daughters in my arms, I do know that I am very fortunate to still be here.

The second philosophy is that with life being so

short, it does not make sense to get hung up on the things that do not contribute to overall happiness and well-being. If someone cuts me off on the highway, so what? Let the person go, and I'll continue living my life the way I want to, and that person will not have any long-lasting effect on my well-being. You should never let anyone hold your emotions and feelings hostage. It is just not worth it.

The third philosophy involves treating others the way I want to be treated. I do not want to be lied to; I do not want to be sucked into petty nonsense or drama. I have had my fair share of all that, and it is just draining. If I am genuine and in good spirits with everyone, I will make not only that person's life a little bit easier and more pleasant, but my life as well.

The final philosophy is that I must be myself and that I should never change for anyone or try to be someone that I am not. With that being said, the experiences that I have endured are a part of me and have given me the wisdom and insight that I now possess. This knowledge is a gift, but it is not the way I would have wanted to acquire it.

I was in survival mode for such a long time. This combined with my new way of thinking has enabled me to don my rose-colored glasses to observe and interpret the world with a fresh perspective. Furthermore, my glasses are unique to me because my experiences were unique. They are a part of my life that can never be undone or take away, nor would I want them to be taken away from me. I will use my glasses all the time now; they will play a significant role in the way I live my life.

These glasses are a gift, diamonds in the rough, oases in the desert, things I did not ask for. Initially, I never thought of these as gifts. But they are because out of tragedy I have grown. And I am grateful for having them. Most importantly, I like to think that my glasses are a gift from Jen, something that I will always have in my toolbox, something I will have for the rest of my life, something that will help me in my life's journey.

28

The End of the Beginning

"Now this is not the end: It is not even the beginning of the end. But it is, perhaps. The end of the beginning."

–Winston Churchill; 1942,
Second Battle of El Alamein.

On the first weekend of November, every year thousands of runners brave the cold, New York City weather by running 26.2 miles that takes them through the five boroughs during the city's annual marathon. It has always amazed me that all these athletes have the stamina, the resolve, and, quite honestly, the endurance to run a distance that to some people, including me, is mind boggling. Every year, though, all these people manage to complete the 26-mile journey, ending in Central Park where they cross the finish line.

In November 2018, when I watched the highlights of the New York City Marathon, with the runners crossing the finish line, it made me equate the journey that I endured to a long-distance marathon with a finish line.

For a year, I was told, and I believed that all I had to do was get to a year; one year without Jen, and when I did, I would feel a lot of relief. Going through the "first of the firsts"—all of the holidays, birthdays, anniversaries, and special occasions as a widower, without my partner—was like a marathon.

Just like a long-distance runner, a widower needs stamina, endurance and, most importantly, the strength to undergo the journey on which he is about to embark. That strength can come in the form of love, comfort, and kindness from a widower's support network, or from friends and family. It can come in the form of physical strength, good health, exercise, or even improved mental health. In either case, a widower needs to be ready for the ups and downs that he will encounter following the loss of his spouse or partner.

Just like with any marathon or journey, there must be an end, some type of conclusion in which he knows that it is over. With a marathon, the runners cross the finish line. With a trip, a person reaches his destination. So, what does this look for a widow/widower? What type of ending is in store for someone like me and my friends in the support group? The key is this: it's not an ending but rather a beginning.

When I battled my depression, anxiety, and the constant flashbacks of Jen dying in front of me, I did not want any sort of beginning. I wanted an ending, an ending to the pain, hurt, and suffering in which I was drowning. It was unimaginable to want to go on, having to live life in such a horrible way. That was the lowest point of my life. But life did go on, day after day, night after night, so that the pain ever so slowly was being chipped away. I knew that I was reaching some type of conclusion, but I seemed to be taking forever to get there. As Dennis consistently said: "Don't rush things, brother." The light at the end of the tunnel was getting brighter in a painstaking way, but the important thing was that the light was not extinguishing, nor was it getting dimmer.

As the weeks turned into months following the day Jen was laid to rest, the physical and emotional pain did ebb and flow. To expect anything else would have been foolish, nor would it have been wise to race through the grieving process. My journey through grief and pain was my journey, and it would not have been in my best interest to have sped through any of it. It would have been counterproductive and detrimental to my own mental health to want to have skipped over any part of my bereavement. There are still plenty of times that I get upset, and yes even cry, as I work very hard to control the raw emotions about the finality of Jen's physical presence in my life. Fortunately, the frequency and duration of the breakdowns have progressively decreased. They still do occur, and just like waves at the beach, they will continue to crash on my shore then retreat. Making peace with the fact that the pain of what happened in my marriage with Jen will always be an integral part of my life has also helped me. It is what has shaped me and can never be undone.

In my line of work, companies that operate

addiction treatment centers conduct a retrospective analysis after a sentinel event, in which there was a risk of harm to someone (e.g., a medical emergency, evacuation of a facility due to a disaster, etc.). The common methodology employed during a retrospective analysis is to determine what could have been done differently so that the sentinel event will most likely not occur again. This is the cornerstone concept of performance improvement—identifying what needs to change so that things can get better.

A widow/widower, especially a young one, could theoretically do the same thing by asking the question: How can I learn from the pain of the past so that I can make the future better for myself? Obviously, to be crystal clear, the widow/widower has not done anything wrong. This does not mean, however, that the individual cannot grow as a person to become a stronger and more insightful individual.

I spent a lot of time looking back at what I did in the year after my wife died, and there were plenty of things that I wished I had handled in a better fashion, things that I wished had not occurred. BUT I am very thankful that first, I have the ability now to actually look retrospectively at my life and determine what my opportunities for self-improvement are. And, second, I am grateful that I am in a place where I can implement those opportunities for improving my life, especially with and for my daughters.

A prime example of conducting the retrospective on my life was choosing to go to the support group. I had a tremendous amount of hesitation and doubt when my closest friends suggested that I attend a group in early 2018. I was scared to go and discuss my loss with a group of strangers, people who had no idea who I was, but nevertheless, my friends persisted in their efforts in getting me to go. When I broke down and started attending the group, I realized it was one of the best decisions I made during my journey.

Now looking back on my decision to wait and attend the support group, I wish that I would have listened to my friends and started going to the weekly groups much sooner. What I learned from that experience is that I needed to be more open-minded, especially when it came to listening to the advice of my friends. They always had my best interests and more importantly, they had the ability to provide a perspective that was not only meaningful and insightful, but also extremely valuable to my well-being.

I've already explained that my new lenses, my rose-colored glasses, are a tool for how I look at the world. It would be naive and wrong for me to say that these glasses were the only tool I acquired following Jen's death. I had become a newer version of myself. I had developed many new attributes and, quite frankly, a variety of new qualities and traits that I never thought I would possess in my life. These were developments in my character that I believe Jen, in some way, was responsible for. These were gifts she was able to give to me even after her untimely death.

I never asked for this new way of thinking…for this new way I look at life. In some respects, it seems fair to say it was forced upon me. Yet, I am extremely grateful. I am forever thankful for every breathe I take on this planet and for being able to walk and play with Giada and Rossella. Even if Jen had not been taken off life support, Jen would never have been able to do those things, because she would have needed the help of machines even to breathe.

I am also honored that I am able to grow and maintain Jen's everlasting legacies—JBF, and more importantly, the way she lives on through our daughters. Whether it is Rossella's cheerful laughter, or Giada's imagination to play house or school, these priceless little women were only made possible because of Jen.

How blessed I am to be able to acknowledge that the world, even without Jen physically present in it, still has a tremendous amount of awe-inspiring beauty—even in those darkest of times when the odds of remaining happy MAY seem insurmountable. For some people it may take longer to find the good and beautiful following a tragedy. That is fine, because every widow/widower's journey is different and should never be looked at with judgement and bias. But the important message: Even when life has kicked you around, you can get back up, multiple times if necessary, and see the positives again. You can remain standing. Even in the gloomiest of hours, the sun will eventually shine and make visible the best of what is.

When Jen died, my life was forever changed in ways that I did not even think were conceivably possible, and I kept telling myself that this was the beginning of the end. I was a 35-year-old widower, with two young daughters, and for quite some time, I felt as though my life was genuinely over. Daily activities presented significant challenges. Child-rearing seemed an impossible feat. It astounded me how in an instant so much could be taken away from me.

How would it be possible to be happy again? How could someone like me enjoy life again after so much I cherished was gone in such a short period? At the beginning of 2018, I would have answered those questions with despair and pessimism. But the world did not stop, the earth continued to spin on its axis, and the weeks and months passed as seamlessly as clouds move across the sky. I had learned to accept what had happened and allow life to move forward. Yes, for my daughters, because they need me to love them as much for their mother as well as for me. Yes, for our family and friends, because the girls and I are an integral part of their lives. Yes, and most importantly, for Jen and my love for her.

It is easy to say that someone must rest in peace but for someone like me—for a widow or widower—those words resonate and have special meaning. It took me a very long time to realize that my most precious gift to Jen is to alleviate her worry about Rossella, Giada, and me. To absolutely allow her to rest in peace, I have to take care of myself and ensure that her legacies, our legacies, Giada and Rossella, grow up healthy and happy.

So, is this the beginning of the end? No, it is in fact the end of beginning. Specifically, my pain and heartache from the period of time following Jen's death, has been coming to an end. And as in any story, this chapter of my life is ending so that I can have a new beginning. The chapters of my life in which Jen was one of the main characters are completed, never to be erased. But there are chapters yet to be written. I do not know how the story will end, but I will always be thankful that I am here to write it.

45641223R00135

Made in the USA
Middletown, DE
18 May 2019